PEARSON EDEXCEL INTERNATIONAL GCSE (9–1)

HISTORY
CHANGES IN MEDICINE, c1848–c1948
Student Book

Cathy Warren
Series Editor: Nigel Kelly

Published by Pearson Education Limited, 80 Strand, London, WC2R 0RL.

www.pearsonglobalschools.com

Copies of official specifications for all Pearson qualifications may be found on the website: https://qualifications.pearson.com

Text © Pearson Education Limited 2017
Edited by Stephanie White and Sarah Wright
Designed by Cobalt id and Pearson Education Limited
Typeset and illustrated by Phoenix Photosetting, Chatham, Kent
Original illustrations © Pearson Education Limited 2017
Cover design by Pearson Education Limited 2017
Picture research by Sarah Hewitt
Cover photo/illustration: **Mary Evans Picture Library:** Sueddeutsche Zeitung Photo
Inside front cover: **Shutterstock.com:** Dmitry Lobanov

The rights of Cathy Warren to be identified as author of this work have been asserted by her in accordance with the Copyright, Designs and Patents Act 1988.

First published 2017

24
14

British Library Cataloguing in Publication Data
A catalogue record for this book is available from the British Library

ISBN 978 0 435 18540 4

Copyright notice
All rights reserved. No part of this publication may be reproduced in any form or by any means (including photocopying or storing it in any medium by electronic means and whether or not transiently or incidentally to some other use of this publication) without the written permission of the copyright owner, except in accordance with the provisions of the Copyright, Designs and Patents Act 1988 or under the terms of a licence issued by the Copyright Licensing Agency, 5th Floor, Shackleton House, 4 Battlebridge Lane, London, SE1 2HX (www.cla.co.uk). Applications for the copyright owner's written permission should be addressed to the publisher.

Printed in Slovakia by Neografia

Acknowledgements
The author and publisher would like to thank the following individuals and organisations for permission to reproduce photographs:
(Key: b-bottom; c-centre; l-left; r-right; t-top)

Alamy Stock Photo: Antiqua Print Gallery 11, Granger, NYC 48, Ian Dagnall 7, Lebrecht Music and Arts Photo Library 37, M&N 36, PF-(wararchive) 76, Photo Researchers, Inc 60, Photo-Lithographed & Printed By James Akerman 35b, Pictorial Press Ltd 18, War Archive 75, World History Archive 67, 95; **Alexander Fleming Laboratory Museum (Imperial College Healthcare NHS Trust):** 90; **Banknotes.com:** 58; **Bridgeman Art Library Ltd:** Bibliotheque de la Faculte de Medecine, Paris, France / Archives Charmet 51, Yale Center for British Art, Paul Mellon Collection, USA 35t; **Getty Images:** Bettmann 23, Daily Herald Archive 92, Fox Photos / Stringer 88, 97, Hulton Archive / Stringer 49, 69, Hulton Archive / Stringer 49, 69, Otto Herschan / Stringer 31, Popperfoto 106, Science & Society Picture Library 84, Science Photo Library 2, Stefano Bianchetti / Contributor 57, Topical Press Agency / Stringer 66, Universal Images Group 16; **Great Ormond Street Hospital:** 38; **Mary Evans Picture Library:** 59, 89, Peter Higginbotham Collection 46, 55, Illustrated London News Ltd 25; Permission granted free with thanks to **www.plaquesoflondon.co.uk** for permission to use their photograph: 78; Reproduced with the kind permission of **East Grinstead Museum:** 100; © **Royal College of Physicians:** 5; **Science Photo Library Ltd:** 12, 29; **The Blond McIndoe Research Foundation Ltd:** 99; **TopFoto:** 65; **Wellcome Library, London:** Copyrighted work available under Creative Commons Attribution only licence CC BY 4.0 http://creativecommons.org/licenses/by/4.0 9, 10; **Out of copyright/public domain:** 50, Radiography and Radio-therapeutics by Robert Knox 80.

All other images © Pearson Education Limited

We are grateful to the following for permission to reproduce copyright material:

Figures
Figure on page 83 from *Edexcel GCSE History B: Schools History Project – Medicine and Surgery* (Bushnell,N. and Warren,C. 2009) p.133, Pearson Education Ltd; Figure on page 103 from *Edexcel GCSE History B: Schools History Project – Medicine and Surgery* (Bushnell,N. and Warren,C. 2009) p.46, Pearson Education Ltd.

Text
Extract on page 50 from *The Illustrated History of Surgery*, Bell Publishing (Haegar,K. 1988) Routledge 9780517665749, The illustrated history of surgery by CALNE, SIR ROY Reproduced with permission of ROUTLEDGE PUBLISHING INC in the format Book via Copyright Clearance Center.

Select glossary terms have been taken from *The Longman Dictionary of Contemporary English Online*.

Disclaimer
All maps in this book are drawn to support the key learning points. They are illustrative in style and are not exact representations.

Endorsement Statement
In order to ensure that this resource offers high-quality support for the associated Pearson qualification, it has been through a review process by the awarding body. This process confirms that this resource fully covers the teaching and learning content of the specification or part of a specification at which it is aimed. It also confirms that it demonstrates an appropriate balance between the development of subject skills, knowledge and understanding, in addition to preparation for assessment.

Endorsement does not cover any guidance on assessment activities or processes (e.g. practice questions or advice on how to answer assessment questions), included in the resource nor does it prescribe any particular approach to the teaching or delivery of a related course.

While the publishers have made every attempt to ensure that advice on the qualification and its assessment is accurate, the official specification and associated assessment guidance materials are the only authoritative source of information and should always be referred to for definitive guidance.

Pearson examiners have not contributed to any sections in this resource relevant to examination papers for which they have responsibility.

Examiners will not use endorsed resources as a source of material for any assessment set by Pearson. Endorsement of a resource does not mean that the resource is required to achieve this Pearson qualification, nor does it mean that it is the only suitable material available to support the qualification, and any resource lists produced by the awarding body shall include this and other appropriate resources.

ABOUT THIS BOOK	IV
TIMELINE	VI
1. PROGRESS IN THE MID-19TH CENTURY	2
2. DISCOVERY AND DEVELOPMENT, 1860–75	23
3. ACCELERATING CHANGE, 1875–1905	46
4. GOVERNMENT ACTION AND WAR, 1905–20	65
5. ADVANCES IN MEDICINE, SURGERY AND PUBLIC HEALTH, 1920–48	88
GLOSSARY	110
INDEX	113

ABOUT THIS BOOK

This book is written for students following the Pearson Edexcel International GCSE (9–1) History specification and covers one unit of the course. This unit is Changes in Medicine, c1848–c1948, one of the Breadth Studies.

The History course has been structured so that teaching and learning can take place in any order, both in the classroom and in any independent learning. The book contains five chapters which match the five areas of content in the specification:

- Progress in the mid-19th century; Nightingale, Chadwick, Snow and Simpson
- Discovery and development, 1860–75; Lister and Pasteur
- Accelerating change, 1875–1905; Ehrlich, Koch and chemistry
- Government action and war, 1905–20
- Advances in medicine, surgery and public health 1920–48; the NHS

Each chapter is split into multiple sections to break down content into manageable chunks and to ensure full coverage of the specification.

Each chapter features a mix of learning and activities. Sources are embedded throughout to develop your understanding and exam-style questions help you to put learning into practice. Recap pages at the end of each chapter summarise key information and let you check your understanding. Exam guidance pages help you prepare confidently for the exam.

Learning objectives
Each section starts with a list of what you will learn in it. They are carefully tailored to address key assessment objectives central to the course.

Extend your knowledge
Interesting facts to encourage wider thought and stimulate discussion. They are closely related to key issues and allow you to add depth to your knowledge and answers.

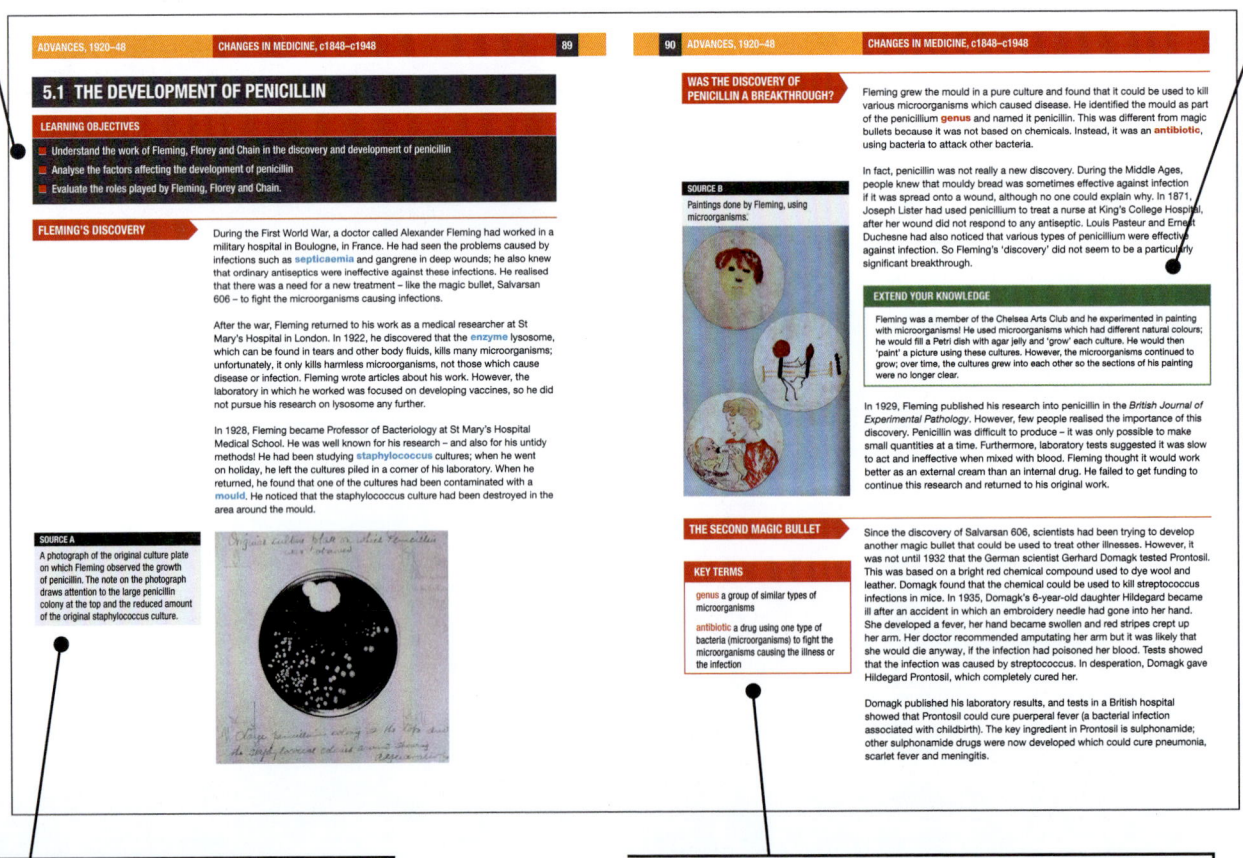

Source
Photos, cartoons and text sources are used to explain events and show you what people from the period said, thought or created, helping you to build your understanding.

Key term
Useful words and phrases are colour coded within the main text and picked out in the margin with concise and simple definitions. These help understanding of key subject terms and support students whose first language is not English.

Activity
Each chapter includes activities to help check and embed knowledge and understanding.

Recap
At the end of each chapter, you will find a page designed to help you consolidate and reflect on the chapter as a whole.

Recall quiz
This quick quiz is ideal for checking your knowledge or for revision.

Exam-style question
Questions tailored to the Pearson Edexcel specification to allow for practice and development of exam writing technique. They also allow for practice responding to the command words used in the exams.

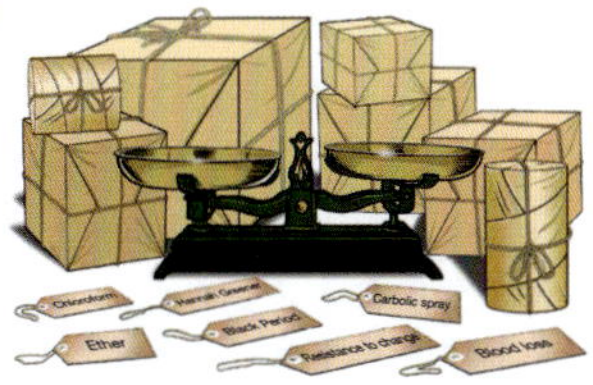

Skills
Relevant exam questions have been assigned the key skills which you will gain from undertaking them, allowing for a strong focus on particular academic qualities. These transferable skills are highly valued in further study and the workplace.

30 DISCOVERY AND DEVELOPMENT | CHANGES IN MEDICINE, c1848–c1948

ACTIVITY

1 Copy and complete the table below about change and continuity in surgery.

	DEVELOPMENTS 1848–60	DEVELOPMENTS 1860–75	CHANGE OR CONTINUITY?
Ideas about the cause of infection			
Problems in surgery			
Dealing with pain			
Dealing with infection			
Dealing with blood loss			

2 In groups of three, discuss one of the following lists of people and factors responsible for progress in surgery between 1848 and 1875. Arrange the items from your list in order of importance, making sure you can justify your choice.
a Key individuals: James Simpson; Louis Pasteur; Joseph Lister
b Scientific understanding (the study of gases and the study of infection); technology (equipment); communication (e.g. publishing ideas in medical journals and meeting other scientists and doctors at conferences)
c The attitudes of doctors and surgeons towards new ideas; the attitudes of ordinary people towards new ideas; the process of scientific enquiry (trial of a new idea, recording results, repeating the experiment, reporting results).
Now form new groups of three, containing one person who looked at each list. In your new groups, discuss whether individuals or factors were more responsible for this progress in surgery.

3 Working in pairs or small groups, model yourselves into 'living statues' where you freeze into positions showing a key moment in the development of surgery in the years 1846–75. See if the other groups can guess which event you are showing.

EXAM-STYLE QUESTION

A01 A02

SKILLS PROBLEM SOLVING, REASONING, DECISION MAKING

HINT
The question asks you about the problems of surgery being solved so you will need to identify several problems and say what had been done to solve them. This is assessing your knowledge, understanding and recall of this topic.

How far were the problems of surgery solved in the years c1848–75?

You may use the following information to help you with your answer:
- ether
- blood loss. **(16 marks)**

Figure 2 Problems in surgery

DISCOVERY AND DEVELOPMENT, 1860–75 | CHANGES IN MEDICINE, c1848–c1948 43

RECAP

RECALL QUIZ

1 Name three different liquids investigated by Pasteur.
2 What did Pasteur say was the cause of decay?
3 Why did Lister think about using carbolic acid in surgery?
4 Why did many surgeons not use Lister's carbolic spray?
5 What does 'laissez-faire' mean?
6 Why was public health in London improved by Bazalgette's work on sewers?
7 What were the terms of the 1875 Public Health Act?
8 How did Elizabeth Garret qualify as a doctor?
9 Why did medical schools and universities not want to accept female medical students?
10 How did Garrett, Hoggan, Jex-Blake and Pechey gain their medical degrees?

CHECKPOINT

STRENGTHEN
S1 Explain how Pasteur's work showed that the theory of spontaneous generation was wrong.
S2 Explain the importance of Lister's use of antiseptic techniques.
S3 Explain how the position of women in medicine changed in the years 1860–75.

CHALLENGE
C1 In which aspect of medicine had there been most improvement between 1860 and 1875?
C2 Why were surgeons slow to accept Lister's antiseptic techniques?
C3 How far did the position of women in medicine change in the years 1860–75?

SUMMARY

- Pasteur's germ theory showed that previous ideas about the cause of disease were wrong.
- Surgical operations were still very dangerous because hygiene remained poor and wounds often became infected.
- Joseph Lister used carbolic acid to kill microorganisms and prevent infection.
- Lister's ideas, and especially his spray, were not immediately accepted by many doctors.
- Joseph Bazalgette created a new sewer system for London which greatly improved hygiene within the city.
- The Public Health Act 1875 made it compulsory for local authorities to provide access to clean water, deal with sewage, remove rubbish and improve housing.
- Florence Nightingale set up a training school for nurses and wrote a number of books about nursing.
- Nightingale also stressed the importance of cleanliness and ventilation in hospital design.
- Elizabeth Garrett faced a great deal of unfair treatment because she was a woman but trained as a doctor and was accepted by the Society of Apothecaries.
- Several other women also wanted to train as doctors but had to go abroad if they wanted a university degree. This was changed by an Act of Parliament in 1876.

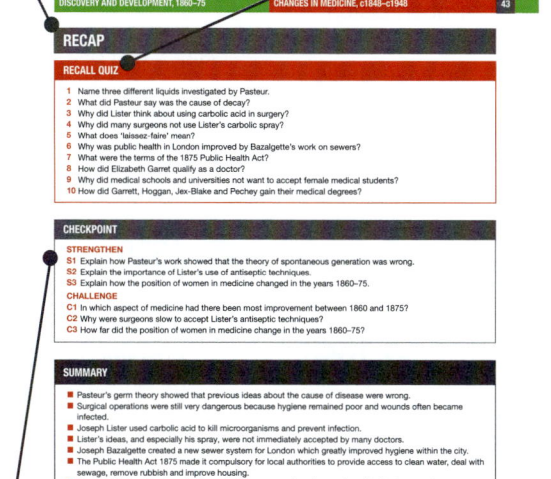

Hint
All exam-style questions are accompanied by a hint to help you get started on an answer.

Checkpoint
Checkpoints help you to check and reflect on your learning. The Strengthen section helps you to consolidate knowledge and understanding, and check that you have grasped the basic ideas and skills. The Challenge questions push you to go beyond just understanding the information, and into evaluation and analysis of what you have studied.

Summary
The main points of each chapter are summarised in a series of bullet points. These are great for embedding core knowledge and handy for revision.

Exam guidance
At the end of each chapter, you will find two pages designed to help you better understand the exam questions and how to answer them. Each exam guidance section focuses on a particular question type that you will find in the exam, allowing you to approach them with confidence.

Student answers
Exemplar student answers are used to show what an answer to the exam question may look like. There are often two levels of answers so you can see what you need to do to write better responses.

ACCELERATING CHANGE, 1875–1905 | CHANGES IN MEDICINE, c1848–c1948 63

EXAM GUIDANCE: PART (C) QUESTIONS

A01 A02

Question to be answered: How far was Lister responsible for the improvements in surgery in the years 1860–1905?

You may use the following in your answer:
- carbolic spray
- X-rays.

You must also use information of your own. (6 marks)

1 Analysis Question 1: What is the question type testing?
In this question, you have to demonstrate that you have knowledge and understanding of the key features and characteristics of the period studied. In this particular case, you need to show your knowledge and understanding of improvements in surgery in the years 1860–1905 and how Lister's work influenced these improvements.

You also have to explain, analyse and make judgements about historical events and periods; here, you need to give an explanation and reach a judgement about the role of various factors in bringing about changes.

2 Analysis Question 2: What do I have to do to answer the question well?
- You have been given two topics on which to write. You don't have to use them and can provide your own topics. (But it seems sensible to do so!)
- You must not simply give information. Think about what improvements these developments caused.
- You are also asked 'how far' Lister was responsible for the improvements in surgery. When discussing these developments, you need to consider whether Lister's work caused each change. The stimulus points for a question like this will usually include one hint that supports the statement and one hint that suggests an alternative.
- The question says you must use information of your own. You should include at least one extra factor, beyond the two topics you have been given. For example, you could talk about the development of aseptic surgery. Alternatively, you could say that Lister's work depended on Pasteur's germ theory and, in fact, Pasteur should get credit for the improvements.

3 Analysis Question 3: Are there any techniques I can use to make it very clear that I am doing what is needed to be successful?
This is a 16-mark question and you need to make sure you give a substantial answer. You will be working against the clock so you may wish to use the following techniques to help you succeed.
- Don't write a lengthy introduction. Give a brief introduction which answers the question immediately and shows what your paragraphs are going to be about.
- Make sure you stay focused and avoid just writing narrative. To help with this, try to use the words of the question at the beginning of each paragraph.
- Remember this question asks about causation. As with question (b), you must make sure your answer explains why each point means that Lister was (or was not) responsible for the improvements in surgery.

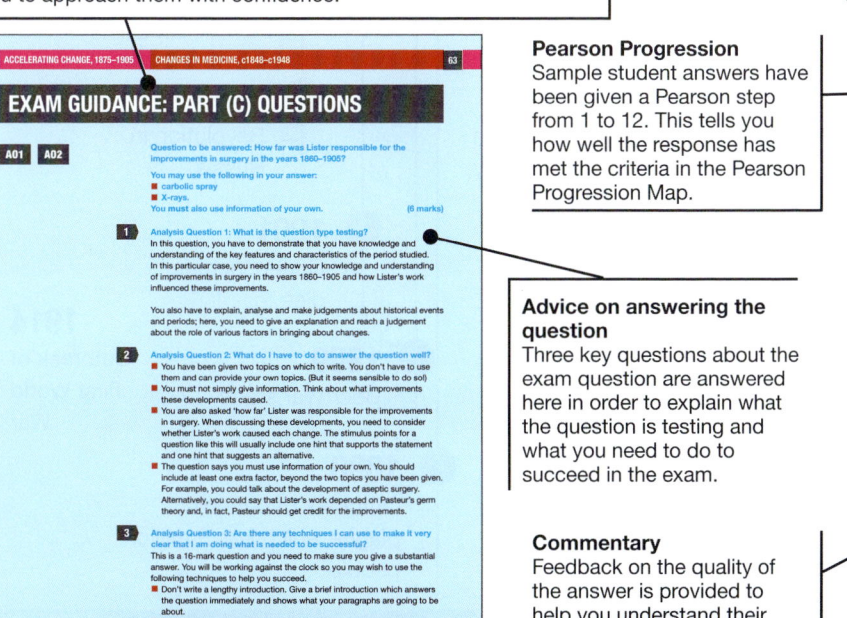

Pearson Progression
Sample student answers have been given a Pearson step from 1 to 12. This tells you how well the response has met the criteria in the Pearson Progression Map.

Advice on answering the question
Three key questions about the exam question are answered here in order to explain what the question is testing and what you need to do to succeed in the exam.

Commentary
Feedback on the quality of the answer is provided to help you understand their strengths and weaknesses and show how they can be improved.

64 ACCELERATING CHANGE, 1875–1905 | CHANGES IN MEDICINE, c1848–c1948

Answer

Good introduction

The period 1860–1905 was one where there were some major developments in surgery which greatly improved the survival rate. The use of anaesthetics had actually increased the death rate because they hadn't solved the problem of infection, so Lister's work developing antiseptic techniques in the 1860s was a major improvement. However, to some extent, Lister's work was based on Pasteur's germ theory and later developments were based on new technology, so Lister cannot be given all the credit for the improvements.

Nice paragraph. Answers the question, gives contextual knowledge and links improvements in surgery to the work of Lister.

Lister read about Pasteur's germ theory and made the link to infection in surgery. He also knew about the use of carbolic acid to deal with sewage and experimented with the use of carbolic acid to fight infection in surgery. He developed antiseptic techniques to keep the instruments clean, to spray the wound and the surgeon's hands while operating, and to keep the bandages clean. As a result, deaths from infection were dramatically reduced. Even though his work depended on Pasteur's germ theory, it was Lister who made the connection to surgery and Lister who experimented and publicised antiseptic techniques, so he deserves the credit for the development of antiseptic surgery.

This is good detail, but you only imply that these developments have nothing to do with Lister. You need to explicitly link the information here to the question about how far Lister was responsible for improvements in surgery.

There were many developments in surgery in the period 1875–1905. New techniques were developed to sterilise the instruments by using steam and the surgeon wore gloves and a face mask to prevent any microorganisms being transferred during the operation. There was also new technology such as X-rays which helped surgeons by showing where bones were broken or if something was inside the wound.

This is a very disappointing paragraph. Landsteiner's discovery did not have much impact on surgery within the timescale of the question. In addition, the answer does not link this to the question, it's just a statement that is vaguely about surgery.

There were also developments in blood transfusions because Landsteiner showed there were different blood groups in 1901. People realised that the blood group had to be matched to make transfusions work.

Good concise finish; this makes a clear judgement about how far Lister was responsible for the improvements in surgery.

Although Lister could not have developed antiseptic techniques without Pasteur's work, Lister does deserve credit for many improvements in surgery in the 1860s and 1870s. The later improvements, such as aseptic surgery, built on his work. However, he cannot be given credit for all the improvements in surgery because new technology such as X-rays had nothing to do with Lister.

What are the strengths and weaknesses of this answer?

The teacher comments show strengths and weaknesses. Notice that the weaker second half of the answer has lots of detail but this is not used to answer the question. If there had been three paragraphs like the one on Lister and antiseptic techniques, this would have been a very good answer.

Work with a friend

Discuss with a friend how you would rewrite the weaker paragraphs in this answer so that the whole answer could get very high marks.

Challenge a friend

Use the Student Book to set a similar part (c) question for a friend. Then look at the answer. Does it do the following things?

- ☐ Identify improvements
- ☐ Provide detailed information about the improvements
- ☐ Show how the stated factor was responsible for the improvements
- ☐ Consider examples that challenge the statement
- ☐ Provide a factor other than the two given in the question
- ☐ Address 'how far?'

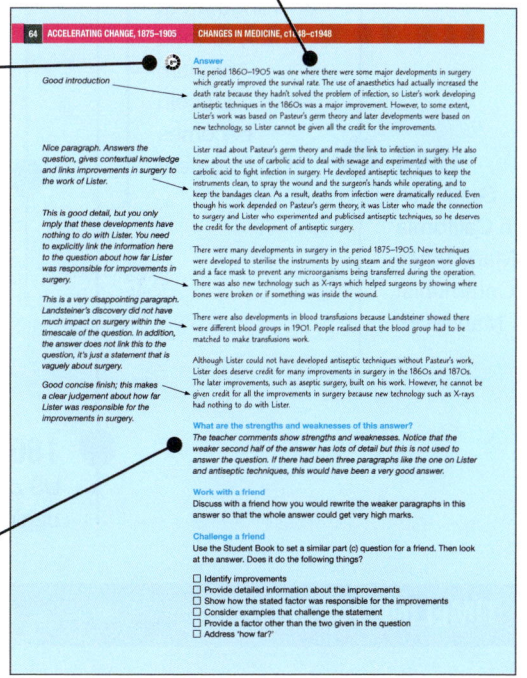

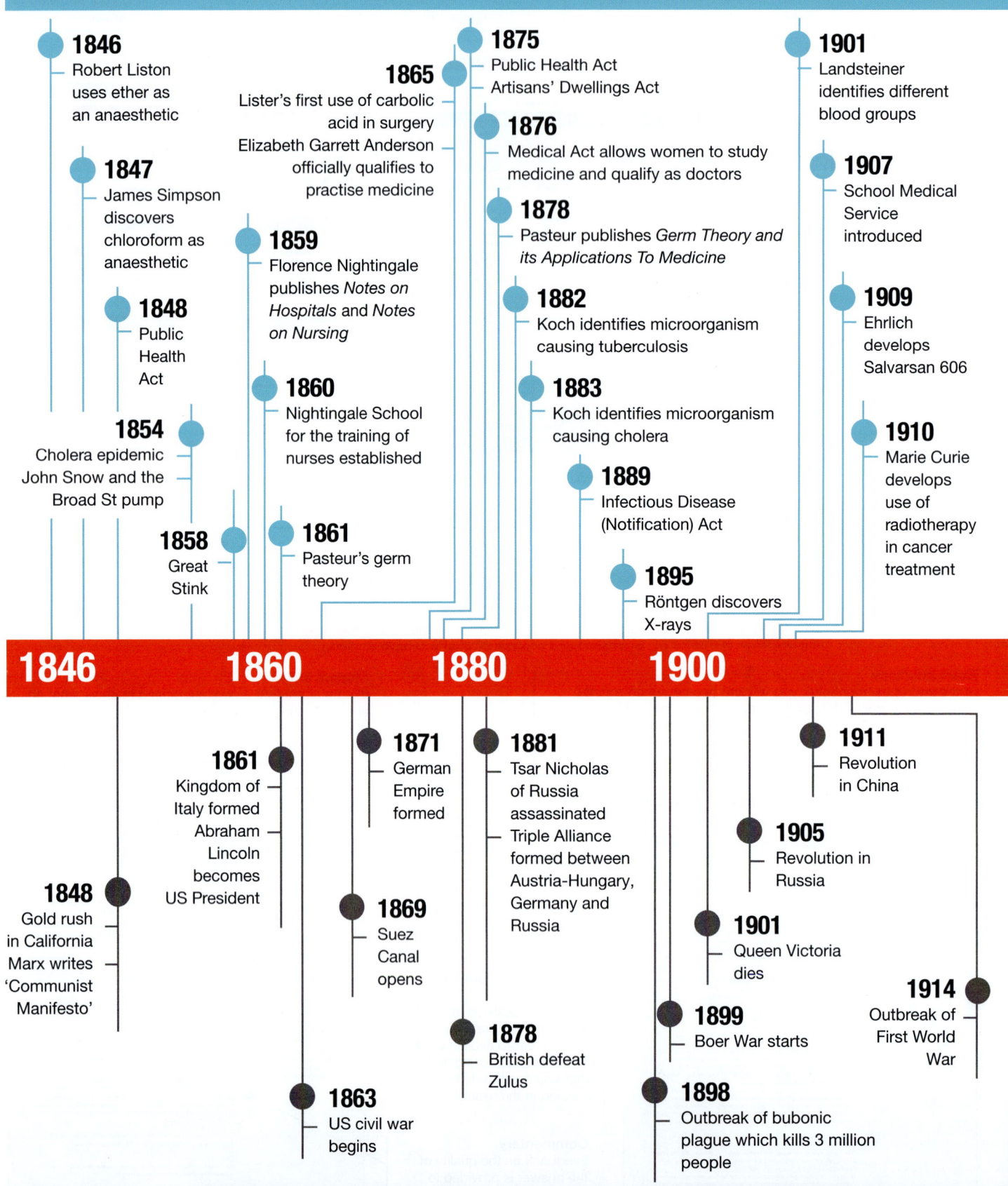

TIMELINE vii

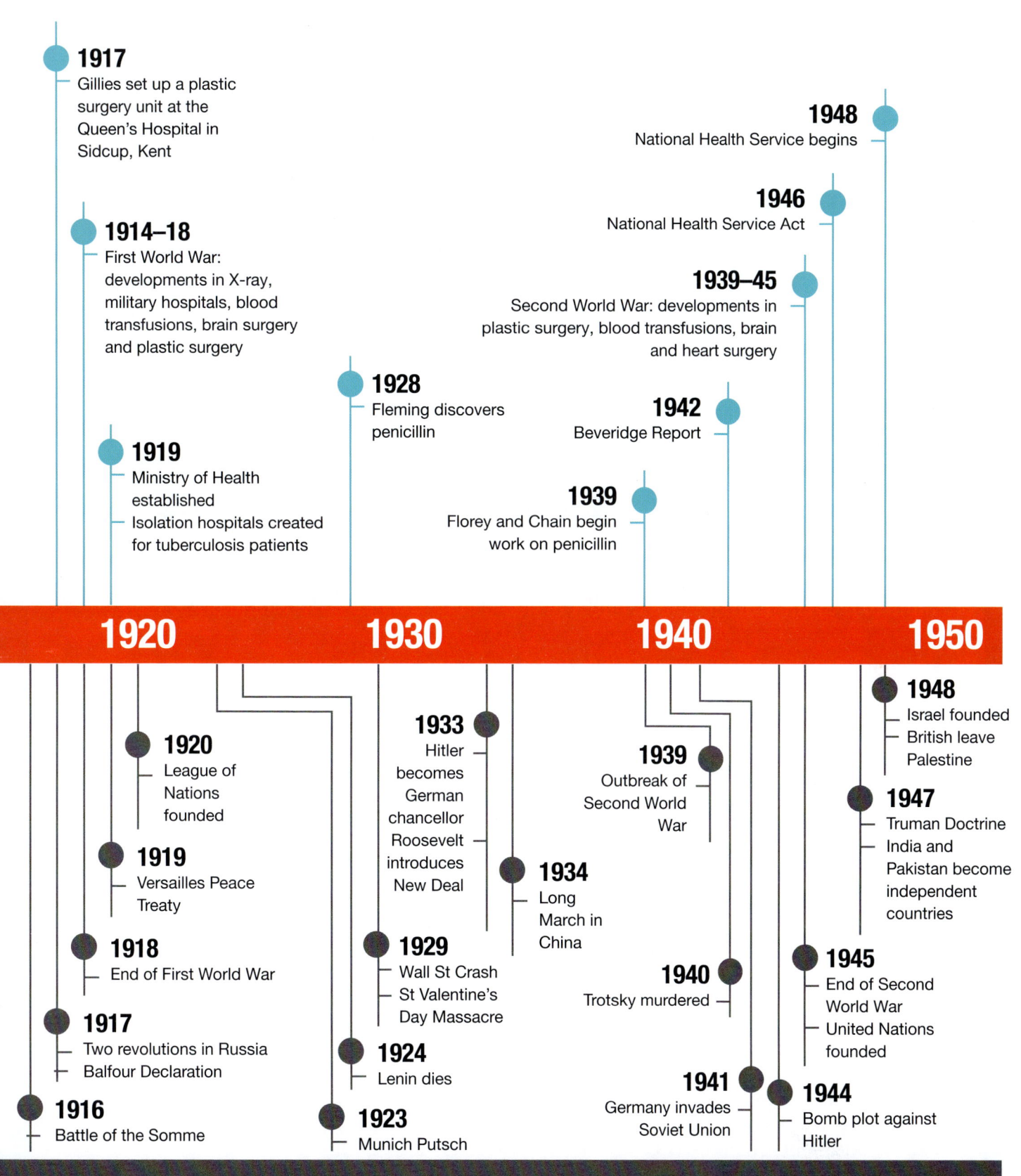

1. PROGRESS IN THE MID-19TH CENTURY

LEARNING OBJECTIVES
- Understand the range of barriers to progress in medicine and in surgery
- Understand the importance of key individuals: Nightingale, Chadwick, Snow and Simpson
- Evaluate the standard of medicine in the mid-19th century.

In the mid-19th century, people did not know what caused disease and they usually blamed it on a problem in the body or on miasma (something bad in the air). This meant that their attempts to prevent or treat illness, either at home or in hospitals, were unlikely to work.

The level of care offered in hospitals was fairly basic and most people were nursed at home. However, during the Crimean War (1854–56) Florence Nightingale took a team of nurses to the British army hospital where they improved the care being offered to injured soldiers. The standard of hygiene in the hospital was also improved and this appeared to reduce the number of deaths from infection.

People's reluctance to go through an operation was understandable. Surgery consisted of basic operations which had to be carried out as quickly as possible because there was no pain relief. Even if the patient survived the operation itself, there was a high death rate afterwards because of infection. The discovery that ether could be used as an anaesthetic, followed by Simpson's use of chloroform, solved the major problem of pain. However, not all the consequences of these discoveries were positive.

Another factor affecting people's health was the standard of housing. In most towns, the quality of housing was very poor and, because many people lived closely together in unhealthy conditions, disease spread quickly. Chadwick recommended various improvements but they were not all implemented. However, the work of Snow showed the importance of improved hygiene and access to clean water in order to prevent the spread of cholera.

PROGRESS IN THE MID-19TH CENTURY   CHANGES IN MEDICINE, c1848–c1948   3

1.1 WHY HAD MEDICINE NOT MADE MORE PROGRESS BY 1848?

LEARNING OBJECTIVES

- Understand that medical knowledge is linked to scientific knowledge and technology
- Analyse the role of factors affecting progress in medicine
- Evaluate the standard of medicine in 1848.

▲ Figure 1.1 The doctor's dilemma

Although there had been developments in medicine in the years leading up to 1848, there were a number of reasons why more progress had not been made.

FOUR HUMOURS

Medical understanding of what caused disease in 1848 was based on ideas that made sense at the time. However, we now know these ideas were wrong. The idea of Four Humours (Figure 1.2) in the body was developed by the Ancient Greeks but it lasted for a very long time because it seemed logical. People knew that blood was an important part of the body and they could see **bile** when people **vomited**. They could also see watery mucus, or phlegm, when people had a cold.

They observed illness and saw that sometimes people became hot and flushed, while at other times they were pale and cold; sometimes people vomited and at other times they coughed and sneezed. It made sense to think that illness was caused by an imbalance in the body's humours but this prevented people from developing a correct understanding of disease. This, in turn, prevented progress in treatment and prevention. Treatments were based on the **Theory of Opposites** (see Figure 1.3).

KEY TERM

Theory of Opposites the idea that if your illness was caused by too much of one humour, the balance of your humours could be restored by eating or drinking something with the opposite qualities

4 PROGRESS IN THE MID-19TH CENTURY — CHANGES IN MEDICINE, c1848–c1948

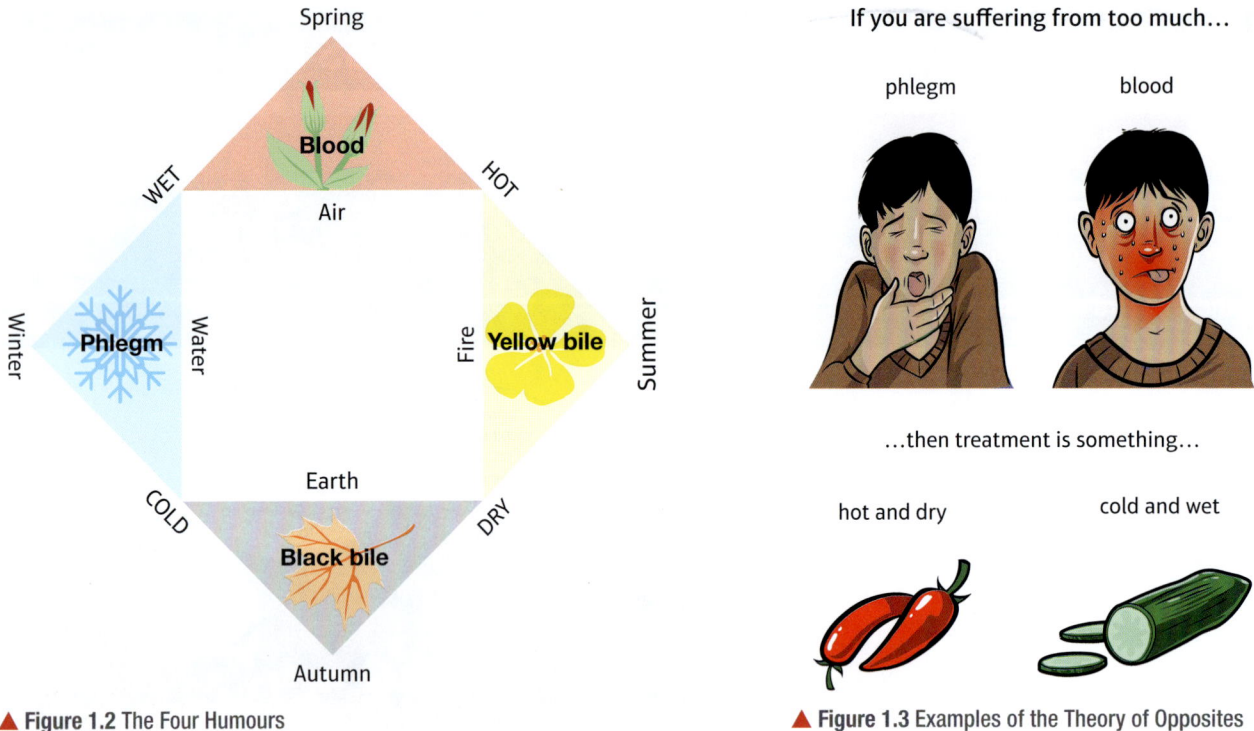

▲ Figure 1.2 The Four Humours

▲ Figure 1.3 Examples of the Theory of Opposites

MIASMA

An alternative explanation of disease was based on the idea of miasma – that disease was carried in unpleasant smells and harmful **fumes** in the air. People understood that there was often a high rate of disease in poor areas, where people lived in dirty, **unhygienic** – and smelly – conditions. They also knew that disease tended to spread more quickly in hot weather. This made the idea of miasma logical: the bad smells (which got worse in summer) were somehow linked with disease.

SPONTANEOUS GENERATION

SOURCE A

From a description of a poor area in London written in 1852.

The water of the huge ditch in front of the houses is covered with a scum. Along the banks are heaps of indescribable filth. The air has literally the smell of a graveyard.

We know that disease is caused by **microorganisms** and we understand that different microorganisms cause different diseases. However, microorganisms are too small to be seen without a **microscope** and, although scientists knew they existed, there was little scientific research being carried out on them at this time. People didn't know about the link between microorganisms and disease; instead, a theory developed, called spontaneous generation. This theory claimed that rotting material (for example, the remains of food, **excrement**, dead animals, rotting vegetables and plants etc.) created maggots, fleas and disease.

DOCTORS' KNOWLEDGE

KEY TERM

microorganisms single-celled living organisms which are too small to be seen without a microscope; they may also be called microbes or bacteria; microorganisms associated with disease are often called germs

Understanding of the body was also limited. Doctors would observe a few **dissections** during their training but most people believed in a life after death and therefore wanted to be buried. The bodies that doctors could use were mainly those of criminals who had been executed. This made it difficult to plan any research on the symptoms of disease or to study particular conditions such as **diabetes** or **arthritis**.

PROGRESS IN THE MID-19TH CENTURY   CHANGES IN MEDICINE, c1848–c1948

SOURCE B

'The Dissecting Room', an illustration from c1780.

EXTEND YOUR KNOWLEDGE

When the number of crimes punishable by death was reduced in 1823, there were fewer criminals' bodies available for dissection. Many medical schools paid cash for corpses, especially if they were fairly fresh. This meant that graves were sometimes robbed so that the body could be sold. Two criminals, Burke and Hare, carried out several murders in Edinburgh in order to sell the bodies.

Lack of understanding of the causes of illness was a key reason for the limited progress in medicine. Because understanding was faulty, doctors' training was also faulty and ideas about prevention and treatment were likely to be ineffective.

FACTORS AFFECTING PROGRESS

- This lack of understanding is closely linked with the level of technology available at the time. If microscopes had been stronger, perhaps scientists would have been more curious about **germs**.
- Other reasons for the lack of progress include the problem of funding for research and the development of new ideas. The government did not feel responsible for issues like this and hospitals usually relied on charity for funding. This meant that little money was left over for research.
- Attitudes were also important. Many doctors wanted to keep on doing what they had always done; they didn't want to have to learn new ways of treating patients. Also there was no proof that their methods were wrong.

▶ Figure 1.4 Barriers to progress

PROGRESS IN THE MID-19TH CENTURY — CHANGES IN MEDICINE, c1848–c1948

> **ACTIVITY**
>
> 1 Make a set of flash cards for the new vocabulary in this section.
> 2 Based on the knowledge that people had in the mid-19th century, which seems the most sensible explanation of illness – the Four Humours, miasma or spontaneous generation?
> 3 Explain why limited knowledge and understanding of the causes of disease prevented progress in medical treatment.
> 4 Discuss with a partner the importance of each of the problems in preventing progress in medicine, then draw a picture or symbol to represent each problem. The size of each picture should reflect the importance of that barrier to progress.

1.2 WHY DID FLORENCE NIGHTINGALE GO TO SCUTARI?

LEARNING OBJECTIVES

- Understand the actions of Florence Nightingale at the hospital in Scutari
- Analyse the impact of her work
- Evaluate the importance of her work.

Florence Nightingale came from a wealthy middle-class background. Her family was shocked that she wanted to go out to work and even more surprised that she wanted to train as a nurse; this was considered a very low-status job at the time. There was no formal training for nurses in Britain so she visited various hospitals in Britain during the 1840s. She then spent 3 months in 1851 at a centre in Kaiserwerth, Germany, where training for nurses had begun in 1833.

In 1853, she became superintendent of a small nursing home in London, called the 'Institution for Sick Gentlewomen in Distressed Circumstances'. However, she had met Sidney Herbert, the Secretary for War, in 1847 and he now asked her to take a team of 38 nurses to work in the military hospital at Scutari. Britain was fighting against Russia in the Crimean Peninsula, in the Black Sea. Many British soldiers were being injured in the Crimean War but a large number of the deaths that occurred were caused by infection rather than the original injuries.

CONDITIONS AT SCUTARI

When she arrived, Nightingale found the hospital was crowded, with almost 10,000 patients in appalling conditions.

- Many men were sharing beds or lying on the floor and in the corridors.
- Their clothes were infested with lice and fleas.
- Diseases such as typhoid fever and cholera were common.
- Many patients had diarrhoea.
- It was difficult to get enough medical supplies (such as bandages and medicine) to the hospital.
- Food supplies were limited and of poor quality.

PROGRESS IN THE MID-19TH CENTURY CHANGES IN MEDICINE, c1848–c1948

- The roof leaked and the wards were dirty and infested with rats and mice.
- Although Florence Nightingale had no idea that this was the case, the hospital was actually built on the site of an underground **cesspool**, where human waste collected. This affected both the water supply and the air in the hospital.

SOURCE C

A painting from 1857 called 'The Mission of Mercy: Florence Nightingale receiving the Wounded at Scutari'.

NIGHTINGALE'S ACTIONS

SOURCE D

From an official report about the state of the army hospitals in the Crimea.

The nurses' duties included washing the soldiers' wounds and preparing for the morning visits of the medical officer; to accompany the medical officer and dress the wounds. They also had to take his orders about diet, drink, and medical comforts to Miss Nightingale. They had to see that cleanliness, both of the wards and of the person, was attended to. We have reason to believe that the services of these hospital attendants have been extremely valuable.

Nightingale and her nurses scrubbed the surfaces clean and washed all the sheets, towels, bandages and equipment. She believed in miasma and the importance of fresh air, so she had windows opened to improve the flow of air. Nightingale and her nurses cleaned the kitchens and improved the quality of the food. A fund of money, a lot of it raised by the *Times* newspaper, meant that she could buy new supplies, including 200 towels, clean shirts, soap, plates and cutlery.

EXTEND YOUR KNOWLEDGE

The situation in the hospital, and Nightingale's work there, was reported in the *Times* newspaper. A wealthy woman called Angela Burdett-Courts was interested in the report. She had already used some of her fortune to provide housing, a school, children's playgrounds and medical care for poor people in London.

When she read about Nightingale's work, she decided to help by providing a £150 drying closet machine, which could dry 1,000 pieces of wet linen (such as sheets) in less than half an hour.

THE IMPACT OF NIGHTINGALE'S WORK

Army medical staff had resisted the idea of nurses coming out to work in the Crimea because they felt that women would not be able to cope with the conditions there. They also felt that the women's medical knowledge was limited; when Nightingale wanted to make changes, they saw her comments as criticism and resented her. However, her habit of making a final round at night, checking on all the patients, gained her the nickname of 'The Lady with the Lamp' and made her very popular with the patients and back in Britain.

Nevertheless, the death rate at Nightingale's hospital was higher than at the other hospitals, even with all her improvements. It was not until 1855, when a government **sanitary** commission repaired the drains and improved the supply of drinking water, that the death rate began to fall dramatically.

ACTIVITY

1 What barriers to progress did Nightingale face at Scutari?
2 Nightingale believed disease was spread by miasma. How does this explain her actions in the hospital?
3 Would she have gained her favourable reputation in Britain if the drains had not been repaired and the water supply improved?

EXAM-STYLE QUESTION

AO1 **AO2**

SKILLS ▸ ADAPTIVE LEARNING

Explain **two** ways in which the situation at Scutari in 1856 was different from the situation when Nightingale arrived. **(6 marks)**

HINT
This question is testing your knowledge by asking you to give two examples of difference. Make sure that in each case, you identify the difference and support it with details about (a) the situation when Nightingale arrived and (b) how the situation changed as a result of her work.

1.3 HOW MUCH PROGRESS WAS THERE IN SURGERY?

LEARNING OBJECTIVES

- Understand the key features of surgery in 1848
- Analyse the reasons why there was a low standard in surgery
- Evaluate the extent to which the problems of surgery had been overcome by 1860.

In the mid-1840s, the medical training course for doctors took 4 years. It included lectures on illness and treatment, practical experience in a hospital, and practical experience of **midwifery** and **surgery**.

KEY TERM

tumour a growth in some part of the body; some tumours are harmless but others can affect the body or even cause death

However, surgical operations were either very basic procedures, such as cutting open a **boil**, or life-threatening ones, such as cutting out a **tumour** or the **amputation** of a limb. Amputation would often become necessary if a broken bone poked through the skin and became **infected**.

THE PROBLEM OF PAIN

Pain had been a major problem in surgery. Before the 1840s, the only types of pain relief available were alcohol, a form of **opium**, or being knocked unconscious. In most operations, the patient was awake and often screaming in pain so the surgeon's assistants, or dressers, had to hold the patient down. The 'best' surgeon was not the one who cut most skilfully but the one who cut the quickest. However, advances in chemistry seemed to be solving this problem.

PROGRESS IN THE MID-19TH CENTURY CHANGES IN MEDICINE, c1848–c1948

SOURCE E
A painting from the first half of the 19th century. It shows an operation to remove a tumour being carried out in the patient's home.

SOURCE F
A surgeon describes an operation before the use of anaesthetics.

The patient is brought into the operating theatre, which is crowded with men who are keen to see the operation and the shedding of blood. She is laid upon the table. She knows the intense agony which she is about to suffer. The surgeon tries to reassure her with kind words and tells her that it will soon be over. She is told to be calm and to keep quiet and still. Assistants hold her struggling body down and the operation begins.

At last it is all over. Faint because of the pain, weak from her efforts to break free and bruised from the force used to hold her still, the girl is carried from the operating theatre to her bed in the wards to recover from the shock.

EXTEND YOUR KNOWLEDGE

Robert Liston was widely regarded as one of the best surgeons for two reasons. Firstly, he was very strong (he could compress the artery with one hand while using the amputating knife with the other). Secondly, he was very quick – his record time for an amputation was 28 seconds!

However, he is often remembered today for a couple of operations that went wrong. In one case, he was working so quickly when amputating a leg that he cut off the patient's testicles as well. In another case, he accidentally cut off two of his assistant's fingers. The assistant later died from infection; a spectator – who was spattered in blood – had a heart attack and died; and the patient died as well!

BLOOD LOSS AND INFECTION

KEY TERM
tourniquet something wrapped tightly around a limb to reduce the flow of blood

ACTIVITY
1. Explain why the lack of effective pain relief was a barrier to progress in surgery.
2. Explain why the lack of understanding of infection increased the death rate among patients.
3. Draw a spider diagram summarising the problems of surgery in the mid-19th century. You could include ideas such as pain, speed, infection and blood loss.

Blood loss was obviously a problem so a **tourniquet** would be used to reduce the flow of blood in the **artery**. However, even when patients survived the operation, a high percentage of them died afterwards as a result of infection.

Many operations were carried out in the patient's home, which was not **hygienic** – although conditions in hospitals were often far worse! There was little understanding of how infection happened and the surgeon would wear old clothes that were already stained with blood and **pus**, rather than spoil decent clothes. If patients were lucky, the surgeon might wash his hands before the operation. Equipment was wiped clean or washed briefly between patients; it was not sterilised. The sponge used to wipe away blood was just rinsed out, and bandages were washed and then reused. In addition, there were often lots of people in the operating theatre, as well as the surgeon and his assistants: medical students and wealthy people who supported the hospital with money would watch the operation, making infection even more likely.

THE USE OF ETHER

SOURCE G

From the diary of a 19th-century surgeon.

1 May 1847

Went to Bartholomew's Hospital and witnessed two operations under the influence of Ether: the first I have seen. The loss of feeling on both occasions was complete: the patient had no consciousness of the operation. But the effect on the patient afterwards was appalling, although brief.

Scientists had begun to investigate the chemical properties of various gases and nitrous oxide (laughing gas) was known to make people unaware of pain, even though they were fully conscious. It was used in dentistry in the USA in 1844–5 by Horace Wells, but it was not considered suitable for a surgical operation. Then William Morton, a dentist in the USA, experimented with the gas **ether** in 1846 and found that it had a stronger effect on the patient.

Robert Liston, in Britain, heard about Morton's work. Later in 1846, Liston used ether during an operation to **amputate** a leg. The people watching were astonished that the patient did not need to be held down and even more astonished when he woke up and seemed unaware that the operation had taken place.

Ether seemed to be a wonderful form of pain relief but there were problems. It sometimes caused vomiting and it irritated the lungs, making the patient cough. Another problem was that ether could leave the patient asleep for hours or even days. The gas was also highly flammable which was dangerous when the operating theatre was lit by candles or gas.

James Simpson wanted to find a better **anaesthetic** and carried out experiments, **inhaling** various gases. He was sometimes quite reckless – on one occasion he tried a gas on some rabbits and, seeing that they appeared to be peacefully unconscious, he was ready to try the gas himself. An assistant persuaded him to wait until the next day, when they found that the rabbits had died overnight!

SIMPSON AND THE USE OF CHLOROFORM

This doesn't seem to have worried Simpson. He continued to experiment and discovered **chloroform** was an effective anaesthetic: he and his friends woke up one morning slumped around the table where they had inhaled chloroform the night before.

SOURCE H

A drawing c1850, of Simpson and his friends waking up after using chloroform.

Chloroform did not seem to have the same **side effects** as ether and Simpson, who was Professor of Medicine and Midwifery at Edinburgh University, used it in 1847 for women in childbirth. Shortly afterwards, he became the official physician to Queen Victoria in Scotland and she used chloroform when she had her eighth child in 1853. Partly as a result of newspaper publicity about this miracle pain relief, and partly as a result of royal approval, patients began to ask for chloroform in their operations and it became much more widely used.

When Simpson died in 1870, 50,000 people lined the route of his funeral and money was collected to put up a statue in his honour. The work of men such as Liston, and Simpson, combined with advances in the science of chemistry, meant huge advances had been made in dealing with the problem of pain in surgery.

SOURCE I

A drawing showing the unveiling of the statue of Simpson.

ACTIVITY

1 Write a letter or a newspaper article describing Liston's use of ether. Make sure you include comparisons with a normal operation so that ether is clearly shown to be a wonderful discovery.
2 Which of the problems associated with ether do you think would matter most to:
   ■ the patient
   ■ the surgeon?
3 Do you think Simpson took necessary risks in order to investigate the effects of gases on humans or was he reckless, risking his own death and that of his friends?
4 Which of the following points is the clearest evidence that Simpson's work was seen as a major breakthrough in dealing with the problems of surgery?
   a Other doctors elected him President of the Royal College of Physicians of Edinburgh in 1850.
   b He was knighted for his services to medicine and when he died, his family was offered a burial spot in Westminster Abbey.
   c Thousands lined the streets for his funeral and a public collection paid for a statue to be erected.

THE IMPACT OF CHLOROFORM

SOURCE J

From a notice issued in 1855 by Dr Hall, the Chief of the Medical Staff of the British Army during the Crimean War.

Dr Hall would like to caution Medical Officers against the use of chloroform to treat serious gunshot wounds. He thinks few patients will survive where it is used. He knows that public opinion, based on mistaken kindness, is against him. However, he feels that the pain of the knife is a powerful stimulant, and it is much better to hear a man shout loudly than to see him sink silently into the grave.

EXTEND YOUR KNOWLEDGE

The problem of getting the dose right was seen in the death of Hannah Greener in 1848. She was a 14-year-old girl who was having an ingrowing toenail removed; this was a minor but painful operation, so she was given chloroform. However, she died almost immediately.

Chloroform seemed to have solved the problem of pain in surgery but there were problems associated with its use.

- The Christian Church was opposed to the use of chloroform in childbirth because the Bible says that after Adam and Eve were made to leave the Garden of Eden, Eve was told childbirth would be painful.
- Many doctors were opposed to its use in childbirth because it was not known how chloroform might affect the baby.
- It was difficult to get the dose of chloroform right – enough to put the patient to sleep but not so much that they died.
- Some doctors felt that a patient who was unconscious was more likely to die than one who was kept awake by pain.
- By using chloroform, many surgeons felt confident enough to attempt longer and more complicated operations, often deeper inside the body.

SOURCE K

Snow's chloroform inhaler, invented in 1848.

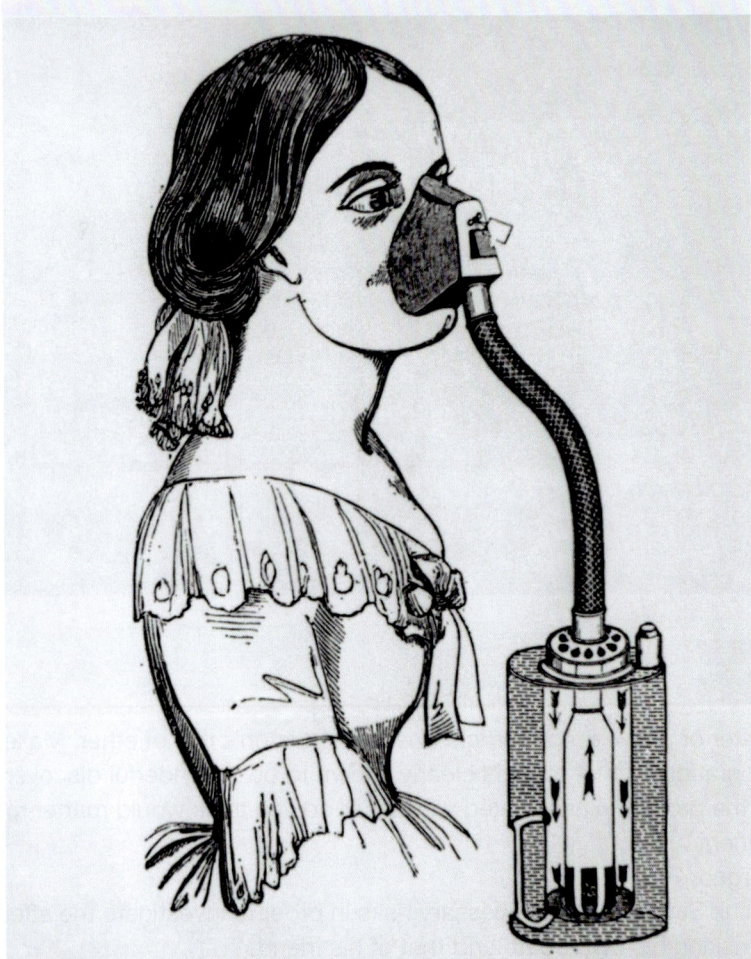

John Snow was able to solve this problem by inventing a chloroform inhaler in 1848. This controlled the dose of chloroform, but the problems of infection and blood loss remained. Indeed, the death rate rose, to the extent that the next few years have been called the 'Black Period' of surgery.

PROGRESS IN THE MID-19TH CENTURY — CHANGES IN MEDICINE, c1848–c1948

THE PROBLEM OF INFECTION

KEY TERMS

gangrene the cells in the body need oxygen; when the blood supply carrying oxygen does not reach cells, they begin to decay and the flesh rots; this can happen if the blood supply is cut off for too long during an operation, or if infection gets into an open wound

sepsis if the body is fighting an infection, the blood supply to the organs such as the brain, heart, liver and kidneys can be reduced, causing the organs to fail and the patient to die; this is also known as blood poisoning

Chloroform gave surgeons more time to work, so they could carry out more complicated operations, often going deeper inside the body. However, they still did not understand **hygiene** and infection. The surgeon's bloody hands and the unhygienic equipment now took germs right into the body, causing infection. The bedsheets and the dressings (bandages) had usually been used before – often, they still had stains and germs on them – and they also passed infection to the patient. As a result, many patients developed **gangrene** around the surgery wound. This infection often developed into **sepsis**, until the patient died. The increased length of operations also caused other problems. For example, if the blood supply to a part of the body was cut off for too long during an operation, this increased the risk of gangrene.

EXAM-STYLE QUESTION

AO1 **AO2**

SKILLS ADAPTIVE LEARNING

Explain **two** causes of the Black Period in surgery. **(8 marks)**

HINT
A cause is something which leads directly to an outcome (in this case a change), not simply something that happened before change occurred. You need to be able to show the link between the causes you identify and the changes in surgery.

ACTIVITY

In groups of four, prepare a news interview for the year 1860. One of you should be a doctor who thinks anaesthetics should be used. Another person should be a doctor who is opposed to anaesthetics. A third person is a nurse who has cared for patients after operations both before and after the use of anaesthetics. The fourth person is the interviewer. All of you will need to know good and bad points about the use of anaesthetics in order to ask and reply to questions and convince the readers. You might want to give examples of operations or include quotes from patients.

▼ Problems and solutions in surgery

▼ PROBLEM	▼ SOLUTION	▼ EVALUATION
Pain	Ether solved the problem of pain but had side effects. Chloroform solved the problem of pain and appeared to have fewer side effects, especially once the inhaler meant that dosage could be controlled.	Solving the problem of pain was a major breakthrough; without this, few people would be willing to undergo surgery and other developments would have little effect. Surgeons were now encouraged to try more complex operations.
Infection	This had not been solved.	The death rate actually rose because there was more risk of infection in more complex operations.
Blood loss	This had not been solved. Tourniquets were used to restrict the flow of blood but there was a risk to the patient if the blood supply was restricted for too long.	This meant that surgeons still could not do lengthy operations.

1.4 PROBLEMS AND IMPROVEMENT IN PUBLIC HEALTH

LEARNING OBJECTIVES

- Understand the problems of public health in 1848
- Analyse the role of Edwin Chadwick and of government in improving living conditions
- Evaluate the extent to which public health had improved by 1860.

▼ The growth in urban population 1801–51

▼ POPULATION	▼ 1801 (thousands)	▼ 1851 (thousands)
Glasgow	77	329
Liverpool	82	376
Birmingham	71	233
Manchester	70	303
Leeds	53	172
London	957	2,362

KEY TERM

Industrial Revolution a period in the early 19th century when the use of power to run machines led to major changes in the way people worked and the growth of industrial towns

Changes in farming and the rapid development of factories during the **Industrial Revolution** had caused many workers to move to new industrial towns in the early 19th century (see Table above). However, houses were of very poor quality because they were built quickly. Landlords felt that workers only needed basic homes and they also knew that factory workers received low wages and would only be able to pay low amounts of rent.

LIVING CONDITIONS

KEY TERM

privy a toilet consisting of a wooden seat over a cesspool

Groups of houses in the poorer areas of industrial towns were often arranged in narrow, dark streets, called 'courts', which could contain hundreds of people. Often a family would live in a single room and 50 people or more might live in one house. Houses were usually damp, with little light or ventilation. In bad weather, the ground floor and cellar could become flooded and a single **privy** might be used by 100 people. Water could be collected from a local pump shared by 20–30 families. The water was often taken from polluted rivers and was only available for a few hours three to five times a week. In these conditions disease spread rapidly.

KILLER DISEASES

KEY TERMS

typhus this disease is spread by body lice; the symptoms include fever, sudden chills, headaches and the patient becoming delirious

typhoid fever a disease spread through contaminated water; the symptoms include headaches and nosebleeds, fever which can last up to 3 weeks, a rash and mental confusion

There were already many killer diseases in Britain at this point. Although a **vaccination** had been developed to prevent **smallpox**, relatively few people had been vaccinated. There was no prevention or treatment for **typhus**, **typhoid fever** or **influenza**. Many patients who survived these diseases were so weak that they died if they caught another illness such as **pneumonia** or bronchitis.

Possibly the most frightening disease was cholera, which killed very quickly – sometimes within a single day. The symptoms involved general pain and **muscle spasms** together with extreme vomiting and diarrhoea, until death was caused by dehydration. Approximately 20,000 people had died in the epidemic of 1831–32.

| PROGRESS IN THE MID-19TH CENTURY | CHANGES IN MEDICINE, c1848–c1948 | 15 |

▶ Figure 1.5 A typical court

DEALING WITH CHOLERA

KEY TERM

local authorities town councils, who make decisions and pass regulations affecting their local area

EXTEND YOUR KNOWLEDGE

Many people also believed that smoking tobacco could protect you from bad air.

The lack of understanding of disease is shown by the fact that the MPs in parliament discussed whether to order a day of prayer when there was another cholera epidemic in 1848. They decided not to do so and instead left matters to **local authorities**, who adopted measures based on the idea of miasma. For example, barrels of tar were burned in the street and people were told to keep warm but also keep clean.

The belief that disease was spread by miasma made it seem that cholera would mainly affect poor people, who lived in very unhygienic conditions. Source L shows an understanding that diseases like cholera spread quickly in dirty conditions. The word 'court' is used to make a joke, linking the type of street and 'King' cholera.

Dr Robert Baker's report on the 1832 cholera epidemic in Leeds described the standard of housing in the poorer parts of the city.
- Many of the streets were bare earth so they became muddy and filth collected in the mud.
- Nineteen streets did not have a **sewer** and another 10 only had a sewer covering part of the street; the sewers had only recently been finished in an area where 30,540 people lived.

- **Stagnant water** created offensive smells.
- In some poorer parts of town, human excrement was collected to sell to farmers. In one yard in the city of Leeds, so much human waste had been collected that it took 75 cart loads to remove it!

SOURCE L

A cartoon drawn in 1852, called 'A Court for King Cholera'.

A COURT FOR KING CHOLERA.

ACTIVITY

1. How many health hazards can you see in the drawing of a typical court (Figure 1.5) and Source L, 'A Court for King Cholera'?
2. Why would these conditions make the miasma explanation of disease seem likely to be true?
3. Based on the level of understanding in the 1840s, suggest ways individuals might be able to protect themselves from cholera and measures that local authorities could take.

EDWIN CHADWICK AND THE 1848 PUBLIC HEALTH ACT

Edwin Chadwick had been involved with the workhouses, places where poor people could go when they were too old or too ill to work and support themselves. The money for these workhouses came from local taxes, called rates, but many people resented spending too much money on the poor. Chadwick had published a report in 1842, called *The Sanitary Conditions of the Labouring Population*. In this report, he had suggested that it would be better to spend the money from taxes on improving the housing and living conditions of the poor and keeping them healthy. This would be more useful than letting them live in dreadful conditions so that they became too ill to work and had to be supported in a workhouse. His recommendations had included providing clean water and removing rubbish and sewage.

At first, Chadwick's ideas had little support but further cholera epidemics, which also affected the middle and upper classes, drew attention to issues of hygiene. The 1848 Public Health Act:
- set up a General Board of Health
- allowed towns to set up their own local Board of Health, employ a medical officer, organise the removal of rubbish and build a sewer system
- appointed three commissioners (people in charge) for the Board of Health; Chadwick was one of the three commissioners and was also made a commissioner for London's Metropolitan Commission of Sewers from 1848 to 1849.

However, the impact of the 1848 Act was very limited. One problem was that the terms of the act were temporary: the Board of Health was only set up for 5 years and ended in 1854. More importantly, the act allowed local authorities to improve hygiene but did not force them to do so. Consequently, some local authorities took no action.

Another problem was that Chadwick was a difficult person, who was often arrogant and aggressive. As a result, he found it hard to get his ideas accepted even though over 50,000 people died in the epidemic of 1848–49. Attitudes were slow to change and many people did not like the idea that local taxes should be increased in order to help the poor – especially when there was no actual proof that disease was linked to hygiene.

ACTIVITY

1. Chadwick was not a doctor and had no medical background. Why was he involved in medical issues during the 1840s?
2. If Chadwick's ideas had been fully implemented, how effective do you think they would have been in controlling epidemics of infectious diseases?
3. Why were his ideas only partially implemented?

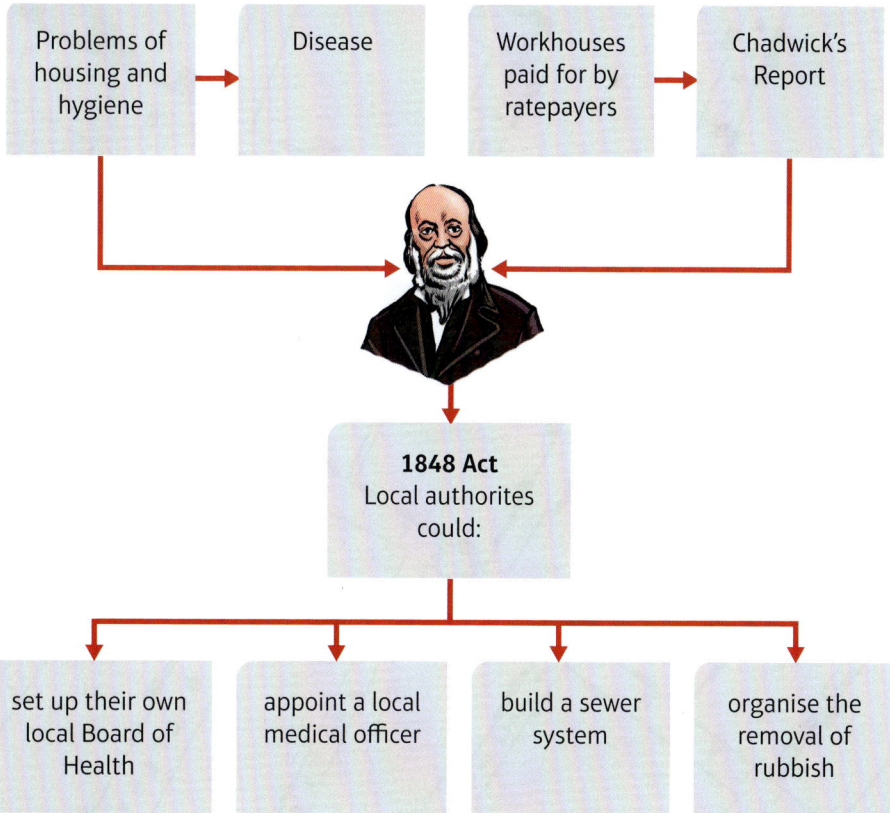

▲ Figure 1.6 Causes and consequences of the 1848 Public Health Act

18 PROGRESS IN THE MID-19TH CENTURY — CHANGES IN MEDICINE, c1848–c1948

JOHN SNOW AND THE BROAD STREET PUMP

Another epidemic in 1854 helped to change people's attitudes. Dr John Snow had suggested in 1849 that cholera was being spread by polluted water. He now conducted research that proved his idea was correct.

He investigated an **outbreak** of cholera in Soho in London using scientific methods of careful observation and records. He made a map showing all the deaths in the area and noticed that they seemed to be centred around the pump in Broad Street.

SOURCE M

John Snow's map of the cholera outbreak in Soho.

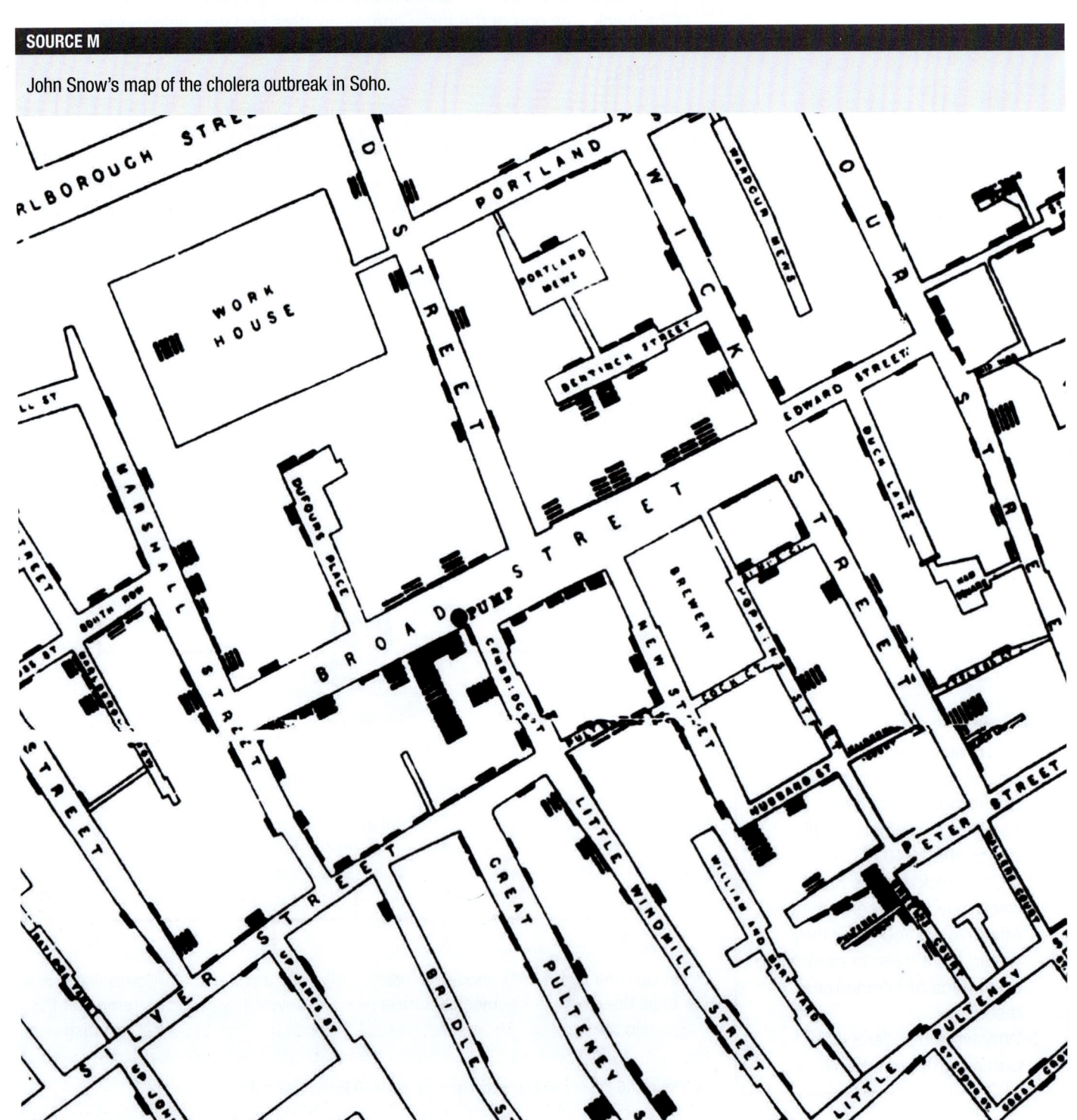

PROGRESS IN THE MID-19TH CENTURY — CHANGES IN MEDICINE, c1848–c1948

▶ Figure 1.7 John Snow's research

1. Within an area roughly 200 metres from the Broad Street pump, there had been 500 fatal cases of cholera.

2. In houses that were nearer to another water pump, there had only been ten fatalities. In all of these cases, the families of the deceased confirmed that they got their water from the Broad Street pump.

3. Workers in a factory near to the Broad Street pump had been badly affected. Eighteen workers had died.

4. Residents of a local workhouse, who had their own water supply, had not been badly affected. Only five had died, out of 535.

5. Workers at a local brewery, who drank free beer, were not affected. The brewery also had its own water supply.

6. A woman living in Hampstead, several miles to the north of Soho, had died of cholera. It was discovered that she had once lived on Golden Square in Soho, and had a bottle of water sent up from the Broad Street pump every day because she liked the way it tasted.

Snow's research was convincing. He explained why some people did not catch cholera even though they lived near the Broad Street pump. He also showed that some people who did not live nearby could still have caught the disease after drinking polluted water from the pump. His theory was further confirmed when the handle was removed so that no water could be collected from the pump – and the deaths from cholera stopped.

Reverend Henry Whitehead worked with John Snow to investigate how the cholera epidemic had started. He found that the first case could have been the baby daughter of Sarah Lewis, who lived at 40 Broad Street. The cholera had caused diarrhoea and Sarah had soaked the dirty nappies in water, which she then emptied into the cesspool in front of her house. When Reverend Whitehead's ideas were investigated, it was found that the brick lining to the cesspool was cracked and polluted water had leaked to the Broad Street pump, 1 metre away.

Snow's work had demonstrated the link between cholera and infected water and this put pressure on the water companies, local authorities and parliament to improve water supplies. However, people still did not know why other diseases spread, because the link between **microbes** and disease had not yet been understood.

Although the link between cholera and polluted water was now clear, very little was done to improve public health until 1858. The hot summer in this year meant that rivers began to dry up. As the level of the River Thames in London began to drop, the rubbish and excrement that was taken to the river by the sewers was exposed along the river banks. The 'Great Stink' was so bad that MPs in parliament actually discussed whether their meetings should be held in another building, away from the river. Realising that this would not solve the problem for the people of London, MPs then passed an act (in the short space of 18 days) to provide the money for a new sewer system; Joseph Bazalgette was chosen as the engineer to design it. However, the most significant improvements in public health did not happen until after Pasteur developed his germ theory in 1861.

EXTEND YOUR KNOWLEDGE

In 1857, John Snow wrote about a small cholera outbreak that he investigated in east London near West Ham. He noted that cases of cholera were reduced when people refused to drink foul-smelling water.

ACTIVITY

1 Which part of Snow's evidence do you find the most convincing in demonstrating the link between infected water and cholera?
2 Why do you think parliament did not immediately pass laws to improve the supply of clean water?
3 Who played a more important role in public health: Edwin Chadwick or John Snow?

RECAP

RECALL QUIZ

1. Explain three different ideas about the cause of disease in the mid-19th century.
2. Name three problems Florence Nightingale found at the army hospital in Scutari.
3. Give three examples of improvements made by Nightingale.
4. Explain three barriers to progress in surgery in 1848.
5. Why did people prefer to use chloroform rather than ether in operations?
6. Why did the use of anaesthetics lead to the Black Period in surgery?
7. What was a court in an industrial town?
8. What were the terms of the 1848 Public Health Act?
9. How did John Snow prove there was a link between infected water and cholera?
10. How did the Great Stink push the government into taking action on the issue of public health?

CHECKPOINT

STRENGTHEN
S1 Explain why a lack of understanding of the causes of disease prevented progress in medicine.
S2 Explain the importance of Simpson's use of chloroform.
S3 Explain why disease spread so quickly in industrial towns.

CHALLENGE
C1 In which aspect of medicine had there been most improvement between 1848 and 1860?
C2 Why were parliament and local authorities so slow to take action to improve public health?
C3 What barriers to progress in medicine still existed in 1860?

SUMMARY

- There was little understanding of the causes of disease in 1848 and therefore it was difficult to make any progress in medicine.
- Florence Nightingale made many improvements to the care of injured soldiers in the army hospital at Scutari.
- Her work was publicised in Britain, drawing attention to problems in medicine.
- Surgical operations needed to be quick because there was no effective pain relief.
- Simpson discovered that chloroform was an effective anaesthetic.
- The problems of blood loss and infection had not been solved so progress in surgery was still limited.
- Edwin Chadwick wrote a report highlighting the appalling housing conditions in industrial towns.
- The Public Health Act 1848 was an important move towards improving public health but its terms were not compulsory.
- When there was a cholera outbreak in 1854, John Snow proved that it was spread by infected water.
- Despite some practical improvements in surgery and public health, medicine did not progress very far as people still did not understand how disease was spread.

EXAM GUIDANCE: PART (B) QUESTIONS

A01 **A02**

SKILLS ADAPTIVE LEARNING

Question to be answered: Explain two causes of improvements in surgery in Britain from 1848–60. (8 marks)

1 **Analysis Question 1: What is the question type testing?**
In this question, you have to demonstrate that you have knowledge and understanding of the key features and characteristics of the period studied. In this particular case, you need to show your knowledge and understanding of changes in surgery.

There is a focus on improvement, so you have to show that these changes made surgery better. You also have to explain why the changes occurred. There must be a clear link between the reason you give for each change and the specific improvement that took place.

2 **Analysis Question 2: What do I have to do to answer the question well?**
Obviously, you have to write about changes in surgery but don't simply write everything you know. You have to show why each change was an improvement and why that change happened. If you just write about surgery, you are unlikely to do this. You should start by identifying an improvement and then providing detail to explain why that improvement happened. If you were writing a plan, your key points would be: identify the first change; why it was an improvement; why it happened; identify the second change; why it was an improvement; why it happened.

In this case, you might consider how Simpson's work in developing the use of chloroform, and Snow's work in developing an inhaler to regulate the dosage, both made surgery better. You can gain 4 marks for explaining the causes of improvement, and 4 marks for your use of accurate and relevant supporting detail. However, if you only talk about one cause, you cannot get more than 4 marks in total.

3 **Analysis Question 3: Are there any techniques I can use to make it very clear that I am doing what is needed to be successful?**
This is an 8-mark question and you need to make sure you leave enough time to answer the part c question fully, as that is worth 16 marks. This is not an essay and you don't need to give a general introduction or conclusion. However, it is helpful to structure your answer as two separate paragraphs, making it clear to the examiner that you are explaining two causes. It can also be helpful to use phrases like 'One improvement in surgery was… The problem was… The improvement was caused by…', 'Another improvement…' and so on.

There are three levels in the mark scheme. At Level 1, you provide general information about surgery and make a simple statement about the cause of improvement. At Level 2, you can explain the cause(s) of improvement and you include some specific supporting detail. To get Level 3, you need to make the connection between the cause and the improvement very clear; you must support your answer with specific details.

22 PROGRESS IN THE MID-19TH CENTURY — CHANGES IN MEDICINE, c1848–c1948

The mark scheme has a range of marks within each level. If you cover one cause of improvement better than the other, your mark will be at the lower end of the level awarded. To get full marks, you need to give a clear explanation of **each** cause of improvement **and** you need to provide good supporting detail.

Answer A
Surgery was very painful c1848. People had to be held down during the operation and the surgeon was expected to work quickly. In 1847, Simpson experimented with the use of chloroform. However, sometimes people died so John Snow invented an inhaler.

This answer does not clearly identify two improvements in surgery, although it implies chloroform and the inhaler made surgery better. There is little supporting detail and it lacks a focus on explaining why the improvement took place.

This is typical of a Level 1 answer: it is about the general topic (surgery) but it has no specific explanation of improvement. The supporting detail, although accurate, is fairly general.

Answer B
One improvement in surgery was the use of anaesthetics. The problem was that surgery was very painful c1848 and so people only agreed to an operation as a last resort. In 1846, the use of ether was found to deaden the pain and meant that surgeons could take more time over their operations. There were side effects to the use of ether and this led Simpson to experiment in order to find a better alternative. He found that chloroform seemed to be an effective anaesthetic with fewer side effects than ether. Simpson's determination and experiments made the situation better for both the patients and the surgeon.

Another improvement in surgery was Snow's chloroform inhaler, which he invented in 1848. One of the problems with chloroform was the difficulty in regulating the dosage and this led to some sudden deaths, as in the case of Hannah Greener. Improvements in technology meant that it was easier to produce equipment and the inhaler allowed the surgeon to control the dosage more accurately, which made it less likely that too much chloroform would be used. This improvement was caused by Snow's desire to prevent deaths from chloroform and improvements in technology that made it possible to produce the inhaler.

This is an excellent answer. Each paragraph begins by stating a change and explaining why it was an improvement. The student has included specific details to show what changed and why each change was an improvement. It would be likely to receive full marks.

Note: this question is only about improvements in surgery. It does not ask 'how far' surgery improved, so there is no need to discuss other problems like the Black Period in surgery.

Challenge a friend
Use the Student Book to set a part (b) question for a friend. Then look at the answer. Does it do the following things?

☐ Identify two changes
☐ Provide detailed information to explain why these changes were improvements
☐ Provide detailed information to show why these changes happened.

If it does, you can tell your friend that the answer is very good!

2. DISCOVERY AND DEVELOPMENT, 1860–75

LEARNING OBJECTIVES

- Understand the importance of the germ theory
- Understand the progress that occurred in surgery and nursing
- Understand the changing role of government in public health.

Developments in science and technology, along with changing attitudes and a change in the role of government, meant that the second half of the 19th century was a period of rapid improvement in various aspects of medicine.

Pasteur's germ theory led to a better understanding of what caused disease. This provided a basis for further improvements in the prevention and treatment of illness at a later stage. Although some scientists and many ordinary people found it hard to believe that disease was caused by something so small that it could not be seen without a microscope, many other scientists began to work on Pasteur's ideas. This helped to bring about improvements in surgery, with surgeons such as Joseph Lister developing antiseptics to prevent infection.

Better understanding of the cause of disease also helped to lead to improved public health and living conditions at this time, through measures such as the Public Health Act in 1875.

A further development in medicine was that, despite considerable opposition, the work of women such as Florence Nightingale and Elizabeth Garrett led to women playing an increasingly important role in medicine.

2.1 WHY WAS LOUIS PASTEUR'S WORK ON MICROORGANISMS IMPORTANT FOR MEDICINE?

LEARNING OBJECTIVES

- Understand how the germ theory changed understanding of disease
- Analyse the role of science and technology in medicine
- Evaluate the importance of the germ theory for medicine.

Louis Pasteur was a French research chemist. In 1854, he was asked to investigate why vats of beer were turning sour. Developments in technology meant that microscopes had become more powerful and Pasteur discovered that there were lots of tiny microorganisms (sometimes called microbes) in the beer. According to the theory of spontaneous generation, these microorganisms were created by the mixture as it decayed. However, Pasteur did not believe this. He suggested that the microorganisms were affecting the beer and making it go sour. He was able to prove his theory when he discovered that these microorganisms could be killed by heating the liquid; if this was done, the beer did not go sour.

PASTEUR'S EXPERIMENTS

Pasteur also carried out experiments on milk, wine and vinegar and he became convinced that the liquids were being **contaminated** with microorganisms that floated in the air. In each case, if the milk, wine or vinegar was heated, it did not go sour.

In 1860, the French Academy of Science set a challenge for scientists – could the theory of spontaneous generation be proved? Pasteur carried out further experiments and publicised his results. In particular, he showed that if he left a mixture in a container that was open to the air, the mixture would go bad; when the mixture was studied under a microscope, microorganisms could be seen in it.

However, if he heated the mixture and then prevented air from reaching it, the mixture did not go bad. This showed that the microorganisms were not created by the mixture as it decayed; instead, the microorganisms were carried in the air and they caused the decay. Pasteur's ideas became known as the 'germ theory' because he said that the microorganisms germinated.

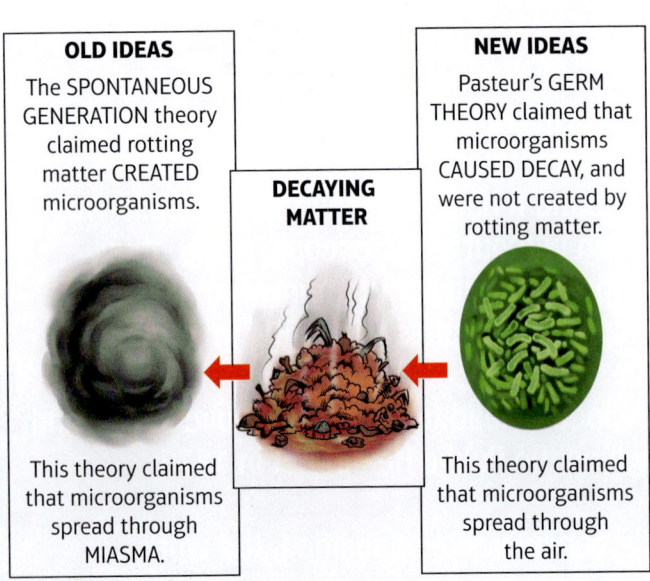

▲ Figure 2.1 Spontaneous generation vs germ theory

DISCOVERY AND DEVELOPMENT   CHANGES IN MEDICINE, c1848–c1948

PASTEUR'S GERM THEORY

Pasteur had proved that the idea of spontaneous generation was wrong – decay only developed if the mixture was left open to the air and thus exposed to microorganisms. He carried out further experiments, such as collecting many samples of air from different places and investigating the microorganisms in each sample. He found the air was 'cleaner' in the mountains and that air from cities contained the most microorganisms.

The usual date given for Pasteur's germ theory is 1861, because this is when he published his experiments. However, his thinking developed in stages over several years and at first he did not make the link to disease and medicine.

Pasteur's ideas were often resisted and even ridiculed but he published details of his experiments in scientific journals. This meant that other scientists could check his findings and gradually, his ideas were accepted.

The four basic principles of germ theory:
- The air contains living microorganisms
- Microorganisms can be killed by heating them
- Microorganisms in the air cause decay
- Microorganisms are not evenly distributed in the air

▲ Figure 2.2 The four basic principles of germ theory

SOURCE A

An illustration showing Pasteur working in his laboratory.

THE GERM THEORY AND MEDICINE

SOURCE B

In this extract from an article published in the *British Medical Journal* in 1875, Dr Henry Bastian explains why he does not believe bacteria (microorganisms) cause disease.

Bacteria... habitually exist in so many parts of the body in every human being... as to make it almost inconceivable that these organisms can be causes of disease. In support of this statement I have only to say, that even in a healthy person they may be found in myriads... the whole alimentary tract from mouth to anus; they exist throughout the air-passages, and may be found in mucus coming from the nasal cavities... They exist... within the skin, not only in the face, but in other parts of the body. Fresh legions of them are being introduced... with almost every meal that is taken.

In 1865, Pasteur was asked to investigate a problem that was affecting the silk industry. He found that silk worms were being killed by a disease caused by microorganisms and he began to make a link between microorganisms and disease. However, it was not until 1878 that he published his *Germ Theory and its Applications to Medicine*. Even then, many scientists did not accept his ideas – hundreds of microorganisms could be seen in the blood of healthy people so it was not clear why some microorganisms caused disease when others did not.

Furthermore, it was not clear how the germ theory could help medicine. Although the germ theory could explain how disease was spread by microorganisms, it did not show how this knowledge could be used to cure disease.

In fact, over the next 20 years, Pasteur's work had a significant impact on surgery because it led to an understanding of why infection often developed after an operation and to Joseph Lister's development of antiseptic techniques.

The germ theory also had an impact on public health because it helped to explain the link between hygiene and health. In medicine, Pasteur's ideas led to the identification of various microorganisms causing disease and this meant that 30 years after the germ theory, vaccinations could be produced to prevent the spread of some diseases, but it was over 40 years before these new ideas about disease led to the development of treatment.

EXAM-STYLE QUESTION

A01 **A02**

Explain **two** ways in which ideas about the cause of disease were different in 1850 from ideas in 1870. **(6 marks)**

HINT

This should not be a long answer. You cannot get more than 6 marks, even if you give a brilliant answer or provide three differences.

For each example, you should say what was different and then provide some supporting detail to illustrate that difference.

ACTIVITY

1. Draw a spider diagram showing how the work of various individuals affected ideas about the cause of disease. Show the four humours, miasma and spontaneous generation as the starting ideas. Then show how the work of Chadwick, Snow and Pasteur affected these ideas.
2. Use Source A to explain how developments in science and technology had an impact on medicine.
3. Write the script for an interview in 1875 where Pasteur is applying for funding. Make sure he explains the importance of his work and why he should receive money to continue it.

2.2 LISTER AND IMPROVEMENTS IN SURGERY

LEARNING OBJECTIVES

- Understand how Joseph Lister developed antiseptic techniques
- Analyse the factors affecting the development of antiseptics
- Evaluate the impact of Lister's development of antiseptics.

As you have seen on pages 10–12, the use of chloroform appeared to have solved the problem of pain in surgery but it had caused other problems. The number of operations went up because people became more willing to have surgery. However, operations became longer and more complex and this increased the risk of infection, especially as conditions were so unhygienic. Consequently, the death rate also increased and the period 1846–66 is often called the 'Black Period' of surgery.

EXTEND YOUR KNOWLEDGE

In 1846, Ignaz Semmelweiss, a doctor working in Vienna General Hospital, noticed something interesting. He realised that the death rate among women giving birth in hospital, where the baby was delivered by a doctor, was higher than if they had their child at home, with only a midwife involved in the delivery. He realised that doctors often came straight from the dissecting room to the hospital ward; he showed that when doctors washed their hands using a chlorinated solution before they entered the maternity ward, the death rate among the mothers dropped.

People laughed at his ideas. He was sacked from his job and eventually he died in a mental institution, possibly suffering from a form of dementia.

JOSEPH LISTER

In 1859, Joseph Lister became Professor of Surgery at Glasgow University. Then, in 1861, he became Surgeon at Glasgow Royal Infirmary, one of the leading hospitals in Scotland. He was put in charge of a new building and hoped that deaths after surgery could be reduced if there was a greater emphasis on hygiene and therefore less infection.

Lister had read Pasteur's work. When he was told that **carbolic acid** was used at the Carlisle sewage works to treat the sewage, he realised the carbolic acid was killing the microorganisms responsible for the decay and smell. He also realised that the smell associated with infected wounds was very similar to the smell of sewage. This made him wonder if carbolic acid could be used to prevent infection.

▶ Figure 2.3 Joseph Lister's development of antiseptics

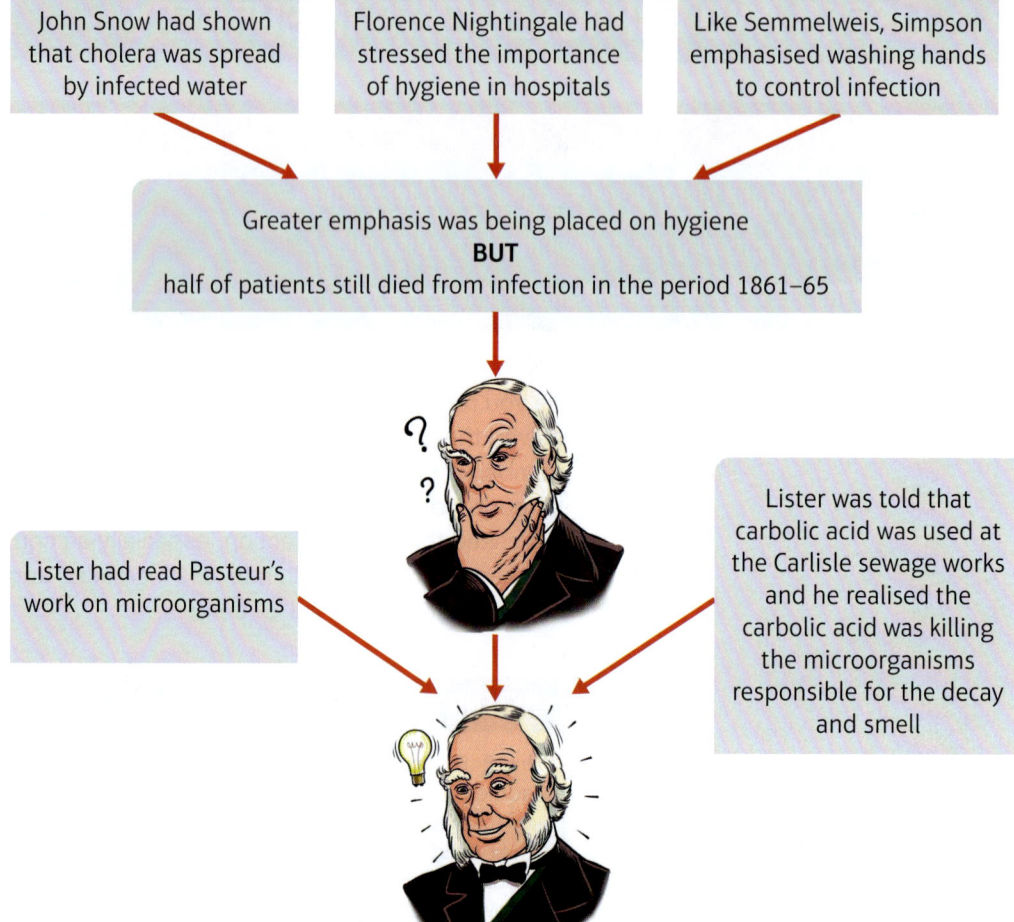

LISTER AND ANTISEPTICS

In one case, an 11-year-old boy was brought into hospital with a broken leg. The usual treatment would have been amputation, because the bone was sticking out through the skin and this would lead to infection. Instead, Lister set the broken bone and covered the wound in bandages which had been soaked in a **solution** of carbolic acid. He was delighted to see the wound healed without infection.

Lister began to use a solution of carbolic acid to clean wounds, equipment and bandages in all his operations, and the death rate from infection dropped dramatically. This method was called **antiseptic** because the techniques were being used to fight (anti) infection (sepsis).

KEY TERM

antiseptic something that will fight the infection by killing the microorganisms

SOURCE C

Figures from Lister's own records of amputations.

Years	Total cases	Recovered	Died	Death rate
1864–66 without antiseptics	35	19	16	45.7%
1867–70 with antiseptics	40	34	6	15%

DISCOVERY AND DEVELOPMENT — CHANGES IN MEDICINE, c1848–c1948

Lister also developed a carbolic spray that could be used during an operation. This was to make sure there were no microorganisms on the surgeon's hands or equipment that could enter the **open wound**.

SOURCE D

An illustration from Cheyne's book *Antiseptic Surgery*, published in 1882. Cheyne worked with Lister and this illustration aimed to show the correct use of Lister's antiseptic techniques to other surgeons.

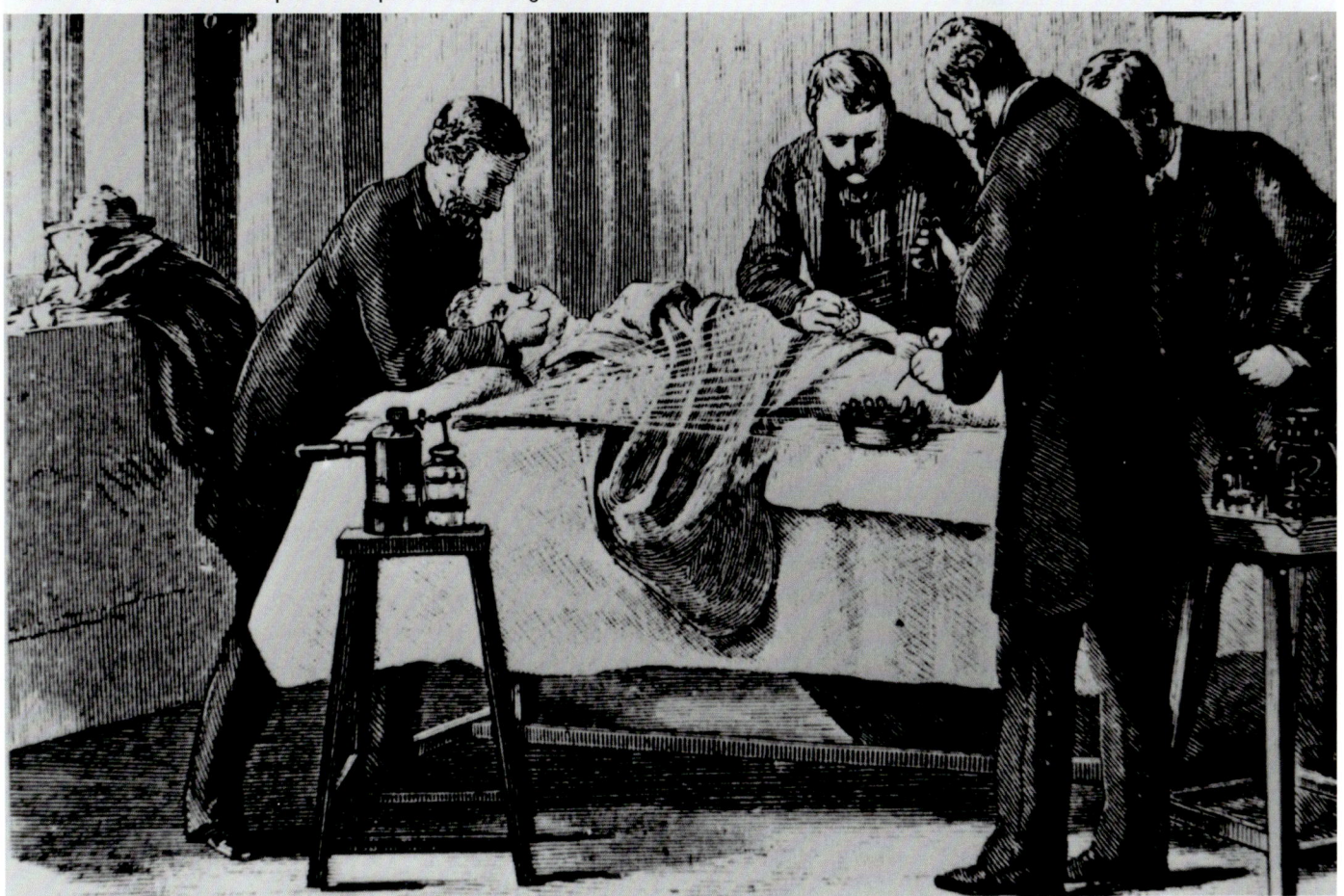

OPPOSITION TO LISTER'S IDEAS

However, there was a lot of opposition to Lister's methods.
- The carbolic spray made the surgical instruments slippery and difficult to grip, which slowed down the operation (remember that blood loss was still a problem).
- The spray made the skin on the doctors' hands cracked and sore.
- Many doctors did not accept Pasteur's germ theory so they saw no need for antiseptic techniques.
- Some doctors who tried Lister's techniques did not use them properly and did not find them effective.
- Many nurses in hospitals were irritated by the extra time and work involved in dressing patients' wounds.
- Some doctors used a simple hygiene routine based on soap and water which had very good results. They saw no need for additional antiseptic techniques.
- Lister himself frequently experimented with adjustments to his techniques. Because of this, other surgeons thought he was not confident that his ideas were effective.

DISCOVERY AND DEVELOPMENT — CHANGES IN MEDICINE, c1848–c1948

ACTIVITY

1 Copy and complete the table below about change and continuity in surgery.

	DEVELOPMENTS 1848–60	DEVELOPMENTS 1860–75	CHANGE OR CONTINUITY?
Ideas about the cause of infection			
Problems in surgery			
Dealing with pain			
Dealing with infection			
Dealing with blood loss			

2 In groups of three, discuss one of the following lists of people and factors responsible for progress in surgery between 1848 and 1875. Arrange the items from your list in order of importance, making sure you can justify your choice.
   a Key individuals: James Simpson; Louis Pasteur; Joseph Lister
   b Scientific understanding (the study of gases and the study of infection); technology (equipment); communication (e.g. publishing ideas in medical journals and meeting other scientists and doctors at conferences)
   c The attitudes of doctors and surgeons towards new ideas; the attitudes of ordinary people towards new ideas; the process of scientific enquiry (trial of a new idea, recording results, repeating the experiment, reporting results).

   Now form new groups of three, containing one person who looked at each list. In your new groups, discuss whether individuals or factors were more responsible for this progress in surgery.

3 Working in pairs or small groups, model yourselves into 'living statues' where you freeze into positions showing a key moment in the development of surgery in the years 1846–75. See if the other groups can guess which event you are showing.

EXAM-STYLE QUESTION

AO1 **AO2**

SKILLS PROBLEM SOLVING, REASONING, DECISION MAKING

HINT
The question asks you about the problems of surgery being solved so you will need to identify several problems and say what had been done to solve them. This is assessing your knowledge, understanding and recall of this topic.

How far were the problems of surgery solved in the years c1848–75?

You may use the following information to help you with your answer:
- ether
- blood loss.

You **must** also use information of your own. **(16 marks)**

▶ Figure 2.4 Problems in surgery

2.3 WHY DID THE GOVERNMENT DECIDE TO TAKE ACTION ON PUBLIC HEALTH?

LEARNING OBJECTIVES

- Understand what the government did to improve public health
- Analyse the factors affecting the improvements in public health
- Evaluate the significance of the Public Health Act 1875.

In the period 1848–60, the work of Chadwick and Snow had shown that there was a link between hygiene and health. The government had passed the 1848 Public Health Act *permitting* local councils to make improvements. However, local councils had not been forced to do this and only about one-third had created a Board of Health. Even fewer employed a medical officer and the General Board of Health only existed for 5 years. Consequently, by 1860 there had been little progress.

JOSEPH BAZALGETTE AND THE LONDON SEWER SYSTEM

However, John Snow's work on cholera and the Great Stink in 1858 did convince the government that the sewer system in London needed to be improved. With this in mind, £3 million was given to the London Metropolitan Board of Works. Joseph Bazalgette became the chief engineer. His plans were carefully thought out and had two key features.

- The sewers should be very large, oval shapes, built of brick, instead of small, narrow, round pipes. Sewage was less likely to get stuck in the oval tunnels.
- The whole system was planned to bring the waste down to the lower stretches of the Thames, where the river was tidal and the sewage would be washed out to sea.

SOURCE E

A photograph of Bazalgette inspecting the construction of the London sewer system.

EXTEND YOUR KNOWLEDGE

The sewer outlets were moved further downstream after the pleasure boat *Princess Alice* sank in the Thames in 1878 and 650–700 people drowned near a place where 30 tons of raw sewage had been emptied into the river only an hour earlier. A contemporary account described 'two continuous columns of decomposed fermenting sewage, hissing like soda water with baneful gases, so black that the water is stained for miles and discharging a corrupt charnel house odour'.

This whole project was extremely expensive and took several years to complete. Most of the approximately 2,000 km of sewers had been built by 1865. They mainly used gravity to keep the sewage flowing but there were also four pumping stations built between 1864 and 1875, and two treatment works to deal with sewage that was not sent out to sea. By 1875, when the project was finished, £6.5 million had been spent. A side effect was the creation of the Embankment along the River Thames in London. This was a way of using the earth that had been dug out of the sewers but it also narrowed the Thames and helped to control the flow of the river.

When the sewers were first opened, a small railway line was installed so people could travel through the sewer system – they could even buy souvenirs.

THE ROLE OF THE AUTHORITIES

KEY TERM

laissez-faire the idea that people should be free to run their business without too much government interference or taxation

At this time, attitudes towards the role of government were changing. Previously, it had been felt that government should take action in an emergency, such as a cholera epidemic, but should not interfere in people's daily lives or their businesses. This attitude is often described as '**laissez-faire**' which means 'leave alone'. Even when a law was passed, people did not always obey it. For example, in 1852, a law had made it compulsory to have children vaccinated against smallpox but it had often been ignored; this was not enforced until a new act was passed in 1871.

In particular, many people did not want the government to start taking action if that would mean that they had to pay more in taxes. However, the work of Chadwick and Snow had highlighted the importance of access to clean water and the removal of sewage. As a result, in 1866, the Sanitary Act said that all towns had to employ inspectors to check on water supplies and drainage. Local governments also began to take action to improve public health. The local council in Manchester made regulations about the size of rooms and the size of windows in new houses, to ensure there was sufficient light and ventilation. Joseph Chamberlain, the mayor of Birmingham, improved water supplies and began to demolish slums. Nevertheless, there were still many problems, as shown in Source F.

SOURCE F

From a report by a London Medical Officer in 1874.

My first impulse was to declare the house unfit for human habitation, and to remove the inhabitants at once. A moment's reflection, however, convinced me that the people being ejected would then have to seek shelter in dwellings even more crowded and in an equally bad sanitary condition.

As the work of Pasteur became known, people began to accept that disease could be passed through polluted water. They realised that access to clean water, the removal of sewage and rubbish, and improved hygiene, would all improve public health. Although several town councils took action, the government would need to pass laws to create a national system of improvements. Previously, the government had avoided interfering but attitudes were now changing. As more people gained the right to vote, there was more pressure on parliament to get involved.

REFORM ACTS

Political parties now began to offer policies that could make them popular with voters and get them elected. This meant they had to think about what ordinary people wanted, rather than only thinking about what the rich wanted.

The Public Health Act in 1875 made local authorities responsible for:
- the supply of clean water

In 1848, about 1 million men, (approximately 6% of the population) could vote for their MPs in parliament. These were mainly from the upper and middle classes of society.

A parliamentary reform act in 1867 doubled the number of people who could vote, including many ordinary working men who lived in the industrial towns where public health was so poor.

▲ Figure 2.5 Changes in the people eligible to vote

- dealing with sewage in a way that would prevent it polluting the water used for drinking and washing
- building public toilets
- ensuring that new housing was built to good standards, to avoid problems of damp and overcrowding
- inspecting conditions in lodging houses
- employing Health Inspectors and Sanitary Inspectors to make sure regulations were obeyed
- creating street lighting to prevent accidents
- checking the quality of food on sale.

This act was hugely significant as it reflects the way that the attitude of laissez-faire was changing and parliament was now passing laws to enforce a national standard of public health. Previously, the standard of public health varied, depending on the attitude of local key individuals. This shows both an increased role of government in public health and a changed attitude towards the government's responsibility for such issues.

The act also shows the way that national government, based in London, had to rely on local authorities in the towns and countryside to implement parliament's orders. Local authorities were now required to make improvements in hygiene and to check that landlords had made improvements to accommodation. Furthermore, the local authorities would have to collect additional money from the rate payers to be able to pay for this work.

34 DISCOVERY AND DEVELOPMENT — CHANGES IN MEDICINE, c1848–c1948

ACTIVITY

1. Look at the terms of the 1875 Public Health Act and rewrite them in order of importance to show which terms would have had most impact on people's health.
2. Why do you think local authorities made some improvements in public health before the 1875 Public Health Act?
3. Draw a timeline for the period 1848–75 and mark the following events on it:
   a. 1848 Public Health Act
   b. Chadwick and the Board of Health, 1848–54
   c. John Snow and the Broad Street pump, 1854
   d. The Great Stink, 1858
   e. Bazalgette and the sewer system, 1858–75
   f. Pasteur's germ theory, 1861
   g. The Sanitary Act 1866
   h. Second Public Health Act 1875
4. Now colour code these events to show the role of government, science, individuals and technology. Several of these events could fit in more than one category – discuss with a partner which category you should choose.
5. Go back to page 16 and study the drawing called 'A Court for King Cholera'. Explain how the Public Health Act 1875 would affect the scene shown in the drawing.

EXAM-STYLE QUESTION

A01 **A02**

SKILLS PROBLEM SOLVING, REASONING, DECISION MAKING

How far was the government (national and local) responsible for changes in public health in the years 1848–70?

You may use the following in your answer:
- the 1848 Public Health Act
- Joseph Bazalgette.

You **must** also use information of your own. **(16 marks)**

HINT
The question asks you to evaluate whether changes in public health were due to government action or some other factor. You need to think about what changes happened and whether they were caused by the government (both parliament and local authorities) or by a factor such as improved scientific understanding or the work of individuals.

2.4 HOW DID FLORENCE NIGHTINGALE IMPROVE HOSPITALS AND NURSING?

LEARNING OBJECTIVES
- Understand what improvements were made in hospitals and nursing
- Analyse the role of Florence Nightingale
- Evaluate the extent of change in hospitals and nursing.

As you have learned so far, there was little progress in public health and the prevention of infectious diseases during most of this period. At the same time, the lack of understanding about the causes of disease meant there was little progress in the treatment of disease or the care offered in hospitals.

DISCOVERY AND DEVELOPMENT — CHANGES IN MEDICINE, c1848–c1948

SOURCE G

A cartoon called 'The Drunken Nurse'.

Most people were cared for in their home by a family member; if they could afford it, they might employ a nurse. A trained physician would visit the patient and prescribe medicine. The nurse (or family member) would make sure the medicine was taken according to the physician's instructions and try to make the patient feel comfortable. The nurse would not have had any training and was not expected to keep records of the patient's condition.

HOSPITALS

Alternatively, people would go to a hospital. These were usually small organisations, relying on charity for funding. They could only admit a few patients, so patients usually had to get a letter of recommendation from a doctor or from a respected individual (such as a religious minister or a wealthy businessman or landowner). Patients were expected to meet certain standards of behaviour and they could be forced to leave if they were rude or aggressive.

SOURCE H

The cottage hospital at High Wycombe, Buckinghamshire.

Local cottage hospitals began to be established c1860. These were usually run by the local **GP** and would have about 12 beds.

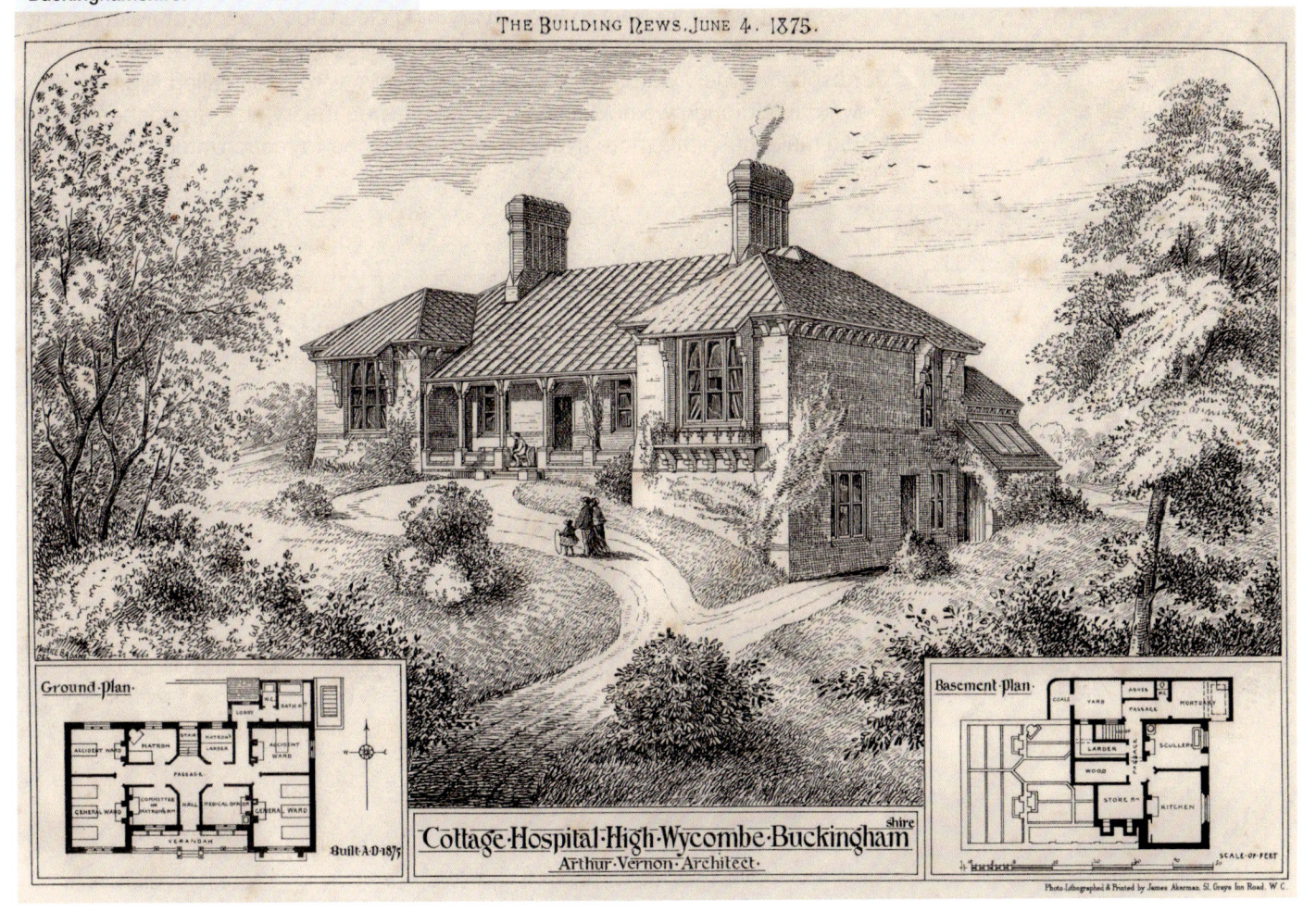

There were some larger hospitals, called **infirmaries**, usually in the cities and large towns. They had **outpatient** departments, where people could queue up to be seen by a doctor. The most important of these were in London. For example:
- the London Dispensary for Curing Diseases of the Eye and Ear had been founded at Moorfields in London in 1805
- the Royal Free Hospital was founded in 1828
- the Hospital for Sick Children was opened in Great Ormond Street, London in 1852.

However, even though understanding of the causes of disease had improved, the standard of care in hospitals was low. There had been little progress in the treatment of disease and nurses still had little or no training.

FLORENCE NIGHTINGALE

Newspaper reports of her work in the Crimea had made Florence Nightingale famous. When she returned to Britain in 1856, she was regarded as an expert on nursing and hospitals. In fact, she did very little nursing personally but she was an excellent organiser and manager. For this reason, she had a major impact on hospitals. In particular, her book *Notes on Hospitals*, published in 1859, set out recommendations for hospitals about space, ventilation and cleanliness.

As you saw on page 7, Nightingale believed in the miasma theory of disease. She felt it was important to keep everything clean, to have lots of fresh air, and to have space between the patients' beds. These ideas were used when new hospitals or new wards were built (these wards were often called Nightingale wards). Although we now know that the miasma theory was wrong, her ideas did make hospitals more hygienic and this helped to reduce infection.

SOURCE I

Ward at Guy's Hospital, London, c1880.

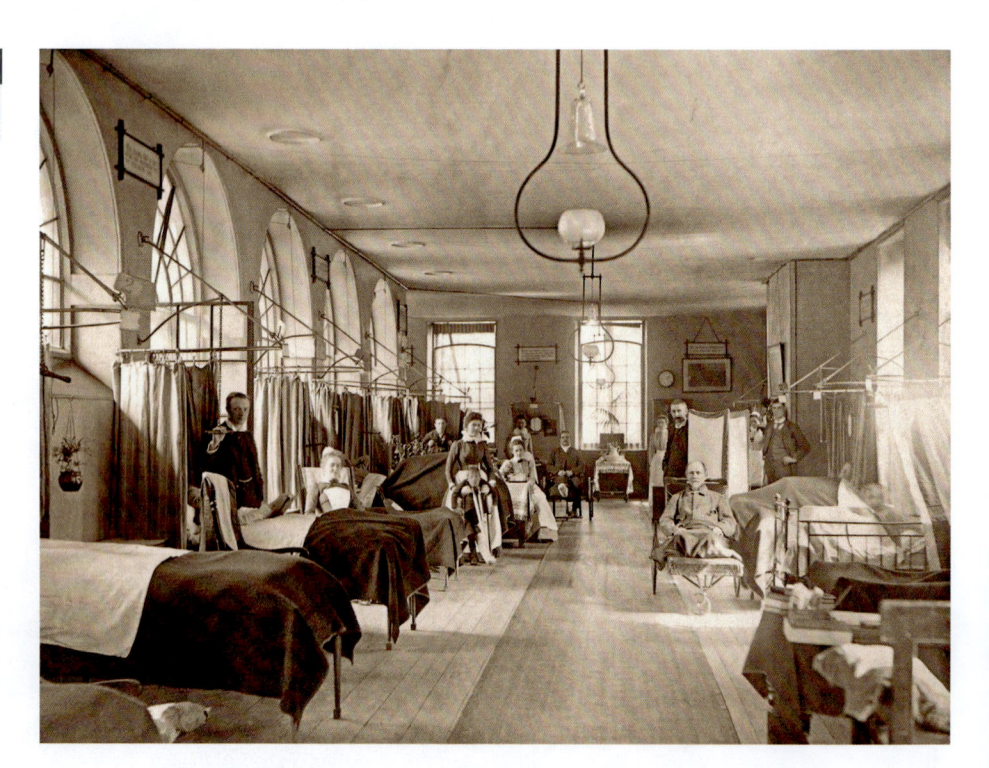

TRAINING FOR NURSES

Nightingale also wrote *Notes on Nursing* in 1859. In this book, she gave advice on the importance of ventilation, light, bedding, cleanliness and food for the patient. She also discussed the nurse's personal cleanliness and the nurse's role in observing the patient and reporting to the doctor. The fact that this book was translated into 11 languages shows that her ideas about practical care and the importance of training for nurses had great influence even outside Britain.

In 1860, the Nightingale School for the training of nurses was established at St Thomas's Hospital in London. Nightingale also helped to set up a training school for midwives at King's College Hospital, London, in 1861.

Nightingale wrote over 200 books on hospital design and nursing. She also gave evidence to parliament and met Queen Victoria. She inspired many others to copy her ideas and high standards, as can be seen in Source J.

SOURCE J

From the diary of Miss Louise Pringle, a 'Nightingale nurse' who went to Edinburgh in 1872 to set up a similar training school for nurses.

8 November

Our head nurse, Mrs Porter, looked quite a dear old lady but her wards were not well looked after. She has been here for 27 years.

21 November

At half past eleven at night we began a round of the wards. We found in nearly all the wards a riot of laughing and talking going on among the nurses and the patients. Nurse Porter's wards were the noisiest; the old lady herself was very loud. Our own wards presented a pleasing contrast and we appreciated even more than before, Miss Nightingale's system. The patients were asleep and the night nurse was quietly in charge.

SOURCE K

Great Ormond Street Hospital in 1856.

ACTIVITY

1. Explain whether you would have chosen to be nursed at home, nursed in a cottage hospital, or to attend a big city infirmary as an outpatient if you were ill in the year 1860.
2. Florence Nightingale's ideas about hospital design were based on her belief that disease was spread by miasma. This idea is wrong. Explain whether this means that her ideas about hospital design were also wrong.
3. Write a letter applying to train at St Thomas's Hospital. Make sure you explain why you would make a good nurse and why you particularly want to train according to Nightingale's ideas.
4. How much did hospitals and nursing change in the period 1860–75? Use the sources and the text to answer the question.

SOURCE L

A hospital ward in Great Ormond Street Hospital c1900, showing the influence of Florence Nightingale's ideas about hospital design and nursing.

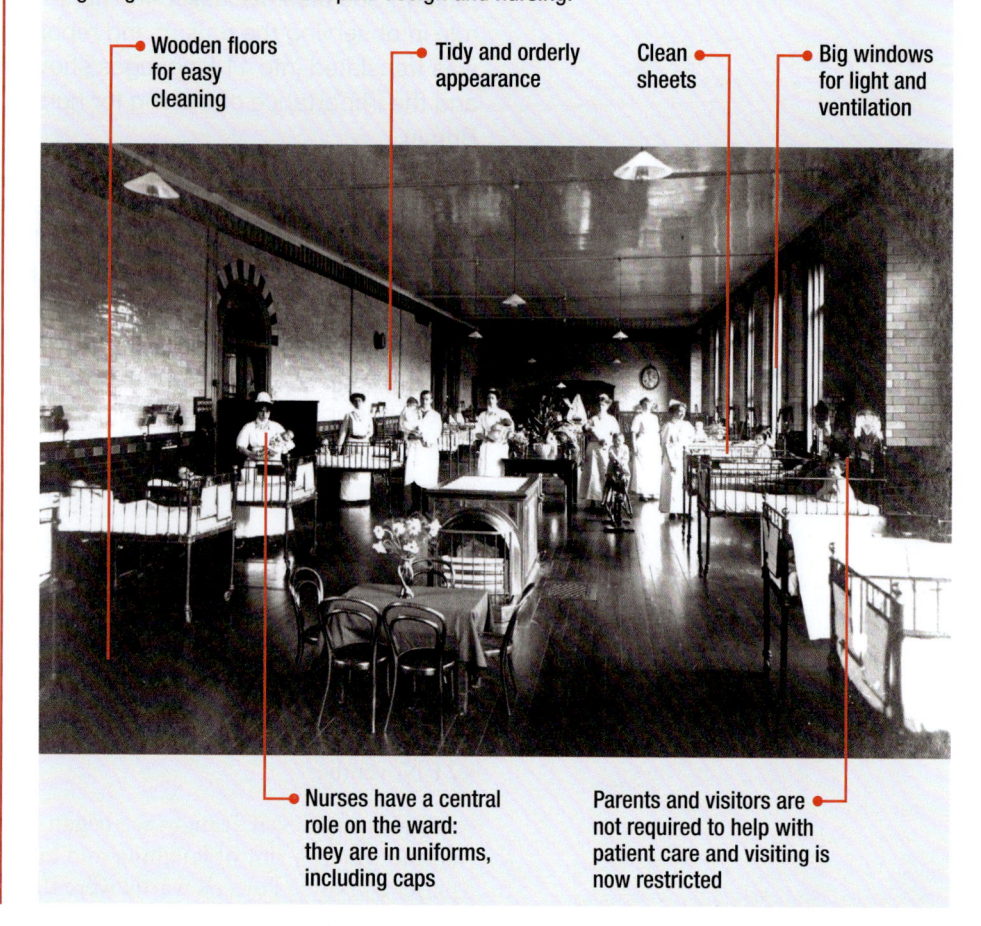

- Wooden floors for easy cleaning
- Tidy and orderly appearance
- Clean sheets
- Big windows for light and ventilation
- Nurses have a central role on the ward: they are in uniforms, including caps
- Parents and visitors are not required to help with patient care and visiting is now restricted

2.5 HOW MUCH PROGRESS WAS THERE IN THE POSITION OF WOMEN IN MEDICINE?

LEARNING OBJECTIVES

- Understand the achievements of Elizabeth Garrett Anderson
- Analyse the impact of her achievements
- Evaluate the extent of change in the position of women in medicine.

ATTITUDES TOWARDS WOMEN

Throughout history, women were usually responsible for the daily care of the sick within the home. Despite this, few women became doctors. This was partly because it was thought that women were not as intelligent as men; this meant that women did not receive the same sort of education. In wealthy families, girls were usually educated at home and expected to be able to play music, sew and paint so that they could be a companion to their husband and make their home comfortable. Girls did not expect to go to university or have any sort of higher education such as medical training.

DISCOVERY AND DEVELOPMENT — CHANGES IN MEDICINE, c1848–c1948

SOURCE M

The motto of a Victorian magazine for women.

We are born at home, we live at home and we must die at home, so the comfort and economy of the home are of more deep, heartfelt and personal interest to us, than the public affairs of all the world.

KEY TERM

suffragist a word used for those who campaigned for women to have the vote

EXTEND YOUR KNOWLEDGE

Dr James Barry was a successful surgeon in the British army, who became Inspector General in charge of military hospitals. However, 'James Barry' was in fact Margaret Ann Bulkley. She had arrived at Edinburgh posing as 'James Barry' and graduated from medical school in 1812, joining the army as a surgeon shortly afterwards. 'He' improved hospital hygiene standards and food and, during the Crimean War, 'he' had a very high recovery rate. It was only when Dr Barry died in 1865 that 'his' secret was discovered.

Florence Nightingale had made it acceptable for women to train as nurses and this fitted in with the traditional view of women caring for the sick. However, people thought that women could not cope with the unpleasant aspects of medical training, such as dissections, and even the desire to train as a doctor was seen as unnatural.

At this time, some women were dissatisfied with society's expectations that they should focus their lives on a husband and a family. Some joined **suffragist** societies and **campaigned** for the vote, while others wanted better education and employment opportunities. Various individuals acted in a way that challenged traditional stereotypes and, because newspapers were now widely read and travel was easier, they inspired other women.

Society's expectations

Options

Education?

Nurse?

Suffragist?

Charity work?

Writer?

▲ Figure 2.6 Increasing options for women

ELIZABETH GARRETT

There were a number of barriers in the way of women who wanted to become doctors. A doctor needed a medical degree from a university or teaching hospital. The Medical Act in 1858 said that doctors also needed to be officially registered with the General Medical Council.

Elizabeth Blackwell avoided these problems: she was an English woman whose family had moved to the USA, where she became the first woman to qualify as a doctor. On one of her return visits to England, she spent a year giving lectures around the country. At one of these lectures, in 1859, she met and inspired Elizabeth Garrett (who later married and took the name Elizabeth Garrett Anderson). Garrett came from a wealthy family, who were horrified at her idea of training as a doctor.

SOURCE N

From Elizabeth Garrett's letters to a friend.

I have just concluded a satisfactory talk with my father on the medical subject. He does not like it, I think. He said the whole idea was disgusting and he could not entertain it for a moment. I asked what there was to make doctoring more disgusting than nursing, which women were also doing and which ladies had done publicly in the Crimea. He could not tell me.

I think he will probably come round in time. I mean to renew the subject pretty often.

My mother speaks of this action as being a source of life long pain to her, that it is a living death, etc. By the same post I had several letters from anxious relatives, telling me that it was my duty to come home and therefore ease my mother's anxiety.

However, it was not to be that simple. She became a nurse at Middlesex Hospital and, in her free time, she also attended lectures that were provided for the male doctors – until they complained.

SOURCE O

A statement by the students of Middlesex Hospital, London, 13 June 1861.

We, the undersigned students, consider that the mixture of the sexes in the same class is likely to lead to results of unpleasant character. The lecturers are likely to feel some restraint, through the presence of females, in giving that explicit and forcible enunciation of some facts which is necessary.

The presence of young females as spectators in the operating theatre is an outrage on our natural instincts and feelings calculated to destroy those sentiments of respect and admiration with which the sex is regarded by all right minded men. Such feelings are a mark of civilisation and refinement.

Garrett applied to study medicine at several medical schools but they all refused to accept a woman student. She then paid for private lessons and even dissected corpses in her own bedroom because she was not allowed to access the dissecting rooms.

QUALIFYING AS A DOCTOR

Complete a university medical degree (this would involve some experience in a hospital attached to the university) → Pass examinations → Be accepted by one of the three medical societies: the Royal College of Surgeons, the Royal College of Physicians or the Society of Apothecaries → Be listed on the medical register

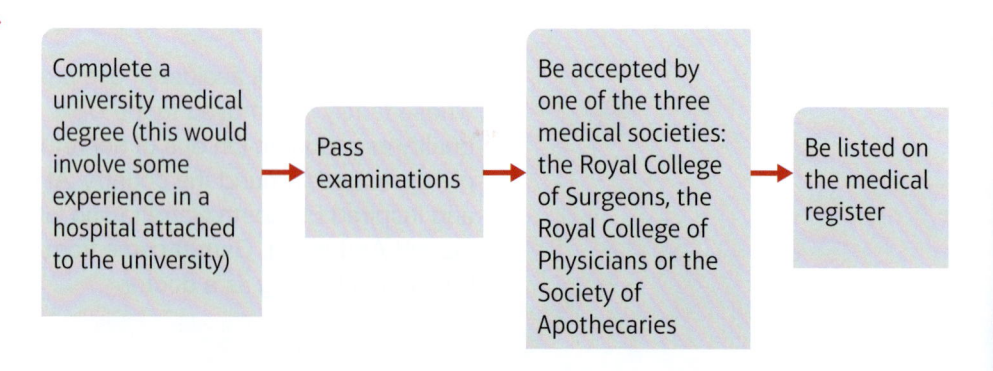

▶ Figure 2.7 Stages in becoming a qualified physician

KEY TERM

apothecaries the people who mixed the ingredients in physicians' prescriptions; an early version of a chemist

Physicians were university trained and could **diagnose** illness and prescribe treatment. However, they could not actually give out medicine. **Apothecaries** needed less training and they could be **licensed** to offer medical advice and prescribe **medication**.

Garrett completed a course of medical training but she could not be licensed because none of the three societies that carried out licensing would accept her as a member. Both the College of Surgeons and the College of Physicians had regulations that stated a woman could not become a member – but the Society of Apothecaries did not. Garrett's father now supported her intention to become a doctor and he threatened to sue the Society of Apothecaries if it did not accept her. This forced the members to accept her and she became officially qualified to practise medicine in 1865. However, the society immediately changed its rules so that no other woman could qualify in the same way.

GARRETT'S ACHIEVEMENTS

Garrett's father supported her again in 1866 when he helped her to open St Mary's Dispensary, in London, to provide medical treatment for women. A short time later, she taught herself French and went to Paris, where she gained a medical degree. In 1872, after Garrett's return to England, the Dispensary added a 10-bed ward, staffed entirely by women. It moved site and expanded several times, becoming the New Hospital for Women, then the London School of Medicine for Women. It was eventually renamed the Elizabeth Garrett Anderson Hospital in 1918, just after her death.

Meanwhile, in 1873, Dr Garrett became a member of the British Medical Association (BMA). She was the only women to be a member for the next 19 years, because the BMA then voted against any further women being admitted. In 1908, she also became the first female mayor in England when she was elected mayor of Aldeburgh.

EXTEND YOUR KNOWLEDGE

Frances Hoggan, a Welsh woman, also studied with private tutors and successfully completed the Society of Apothecaries' examinations in January 1867. However, the society's change of rules meant she was not accepted. She immediately went to Zurich University (the only one in Europe to accept female medical students at that point) and graduated in 1870. She did postgraduate work at medical schools in Vienna, Prague and Paris before returning to Britain. She was eventually licensed to practise in Britain in 1877.

OTHER FEMALE DOCTORS

Elizabeth Garrett and Frances Hoggan were not the only women attempting to qualify as doctors. Sophia Jex-Blake led four other women who persuaded Edinburgh University to let them study medicine. They had to pay additional fees to cover the cost of being taught separately from the male students. They also faced opposition and **harassment** from the other students and they were not allowed to do practical work. When Edith Pechey won a prize in chemistry, it was given to the male student who came second. Then, in 1874, the university decided to force the female students to leave, claiming it had not had the authority to admit female students when they were accepted in 1869.

SOURCE P

An extract from Sophia Jex-Blake's book *Medical Education of Women* (published in 1878) in which she describes her own experiences at Edinburgh University. This extract is about the women students' attempt to sit the anatomy examination.

On the afternoon of Friday 18th November 1870, we women walked to the Surgeon's Hall. As soon as we came to the Surgeon's Hall we saw a dense mob filling up the road in front. Not a single policeman was visible though the crowd was sufficient to stop all the traffic for an hour. We walked up to the gates, which remained open until we came within a yard of them, when they were slammed in our faces by a number of young men.

SOURCE Q

From a speech in the House of Commons on 3 March 1875. The MP is arguing in favour of allowing women to qualify as doctors.

You may talk for a month; you may bring great law to bear upon this question; you may quote great names in history, arts and sciences. But you cannot rub out the stain which will be on the name of this House of Commons if it refuses to do justice for women and if it prevents them from using their own intelligence in a fair, honest and upright manner for their own good.

ACTIVITY

1. Write a report to the authorities of the Middlesex Hospital, summarising the objections of the medical students in Source O.
2. Create a timeline showing the progress of women in medicine.
3. Explain the importance of each of the following in women's struggle to be accepted as doctors:
   - personal determination
   - the attitudes of the medical profession and societies
   - the attitudes of society and parliament.

Eventually both Sophia Jex-Blake and Edith Pechey gained their medical degrees abroad, just as Elizabeth Blackwell, Frances Hoggan and Elizabeth Garrett had done.

Attitudes were slow to change. Although some people were in favour of allowing women medical students to qualify as doctors (as can be seen in Source Q), many within the medical profession continued to oppose this.

SOURCE R

An extract from an article in the medical journal *The Lancet* from 1876.

If those women who are seeking, at an extravagant cost of time and money, to enter the medical profession, were content to work in the only department of the medical profession open to them – namely as midwives and nurses – no objections could be fairly raised, provided they always practised under the supervision of qualified medical practitioners. But the female medical students in London are striving to be placed upon the Medical Register and then to please themselves what branches of medicine they shall engage in.

Eventually, in 1876, an Act of Parliament said that universities and medical societies should accept women medical students and allow them to become doctors. Even so, numbers remained low. The table below shows statistics based on details from various records; although the figures are not always complete, they do show how slowly the number of female doctors increased.

	FEMALE DOCTORS	MALE DOCTORS	FEMALE STUDENTS	MALE STUDENTS
1861	0	2,385	1	3,566
1871	2	Not known	5	Not known
1881	25	15,091	64	5,991
1891	65	Not known	Not known	Not known

EXAM-STYLE QUESTION

AO1 AO2

SKILLS PROBLEM SOLVING, REASONING, DECISION MAKING

How far did the role of women in medicine change in the years 1848–75?

You may use the following information to help you with your answer:
- Florence Nightingale and nursing
- Elizabeth Garrett.

You **must** also use information of your own. **(16 marks)**

HINT

This question is asking about change but it is also asking you to evaluate the extent of change. You will need to provide examples of both change and continuity in the roles of women in medicine and then weigh the two sides of the issue in order to make a judgement.

DISCOVERY AND DEVELOPMENT — CHANGES IN MEDICINE, c1848–c1948

RECAP

RECALL QUIZ

1. Name three different liquids investigated by Pasteur.
2. What did Pasteur say was the cause of decay?
3. Why did Lister think about using carbolic acid in surgery?
4. Why did many surgeons not use Lister's carbolic spray?
5. What does 'laissez-faire' mean?
6. Why was public health in London improved by Bazalgette's work on sewers?
7. What were the terms of the 1875 Public Health Act?
8. How did Elizabeth Garret qualify as a doctor?
9. Why did medical schools and universities not want to accept female medical students?
10. How did Garrett, Hoggan, Jex-Blake and Pechey gain their medical degrees?

CHECKPOINT

STRENGTHEN

S1 Explain how Pasteur's work showed that the theory of spontaneous generation was wrong.
S2 Explain the importance of Lister's use of antiseptic techniques.
S3 Explain how the position of women in medicine changed in the years 1860–75.

CHALLENGE

C1 In which aspect of medicine had there been most improvement between 1860 and 1875?
C2 Why were surgeons slow to accept Lister's antiseptic techniques?
C3 How far did the position of women in medicine change in the years 1860–75?

SUMMARY

- Pasteur's germ theory showed that previous ideas about the cause of disease were wrong.
- Surgical operations were still very dangerous because hygiene remained poor and wounds often became infected.
- Joseph Lister used carbolic acid to kill microorganisms and prevent infection.
- Lister's ideas, and especially his spray, were not immediately accepted by many doctors.
- Joseph Bazalgette created a new sewer system for London which greatly improved hygiene within the city.
- The Public Health Act 1875 made it compulsory for local authorities to provide access to clean water, deal with sewage, remove rubbish and improve housing.
- Florence Nightingale set up a training school for nurses and wrote a number of books about nursing.
- Nightingale also stressed the importance of cleanliness and ventilation in hospital design.
- Elizabeth Garrett faced a great deal of unfair treatment because she was a woman but trained as a doctor and was accepted by the Society of Apothecaries.
- Several other women also wanted to train as doctors but had to go abroad if they wanted a university degree. This was changed by an Act of Parliament in 1876.

EXAM GUIDANCE: PART (A) QUESTIONS

A01 **A02**

Question to be answered: Explain two ways in which nursing in the years 1860–75 was different from nursing in the years 1848–60. (6 marks)

1 **Analysis Question 1: What is the question type testing?**
In this question, you have to demonstrate that you have knowledge and understanding of the key features and characteristics of the period studied. In this particular case, you need to show your knowledge and understanding of nursing.

You also have to explain, analyse and make judgements about historical events and periods to explain ways in which there were differences between those events/periods.

2 **Analysis Question 2: What do I have to do to answer the question well?**
Obviously, you have to write about nursing but don't simply write everything you know. You have to identify two differences and provide detail showing the ways in which nursing in one period was different from nursing in the other period. If you just write about nursing, you are unlikely to do this clearly. You should start by identifying ways in which the two periods are different; then provide detail from each period to show these differences. If you were planning this answer, your key points would be: first difference; details about this difference from 1848–60; details about this difference from 1860–75; second difference; details about this difference from each period.

In this case, you might consider how nurses were trained and what work they did. You will get 1 mark for each difference you identify, one mark for explaining that difference and another mark for detail.

3 **Analysis Question 3: Are there any techniques I can use to make it very clear that I am doing what is needed to be successful?**
This is a 6-mark question and you need to make sure you leave enough time to answer the other two questions fully (they are worth 24 marks in total). This is not an essay and you don't need to give a general introduction or conclusion. However, it is helpful to structure your answer as two separate paragraphs, making it clear to the examiner that you are explaining two differences. It can be helpful to use phrases like 'One difference was…', 'Another difference was…'. You will get a maximum of 3 marks for each difference you explain, so make sure your answer mentions two differences.

Note: The question does not ask 'How different', so you do not have to point out similarities and differences. Just talk about differences.

DISCOVERY AND DEVELOPMENT CHANGES IN MEDICINE, c1848–c1948

Answer A

Florence Nightingale went out to the military hospital at Scutari, during the Crimean War and she made a lot of changes to improve the situation there. When she came back to England, she set up a training school for nurses and wrote many books about hospitals and nursing; her work led to many changes and therefore the work and training of nurses was different in the years 1860–75 from the years 1848–60.

This answer states that the work and training for nurses was different in the two time periods but it does not say exactly what was different. There is little supporting detail and it is mainly about Nightingale rather than the differences in nursing.

This is typical of a Level 1 answer: it is about the general topic (nursing) but it has no specific examples of what was different. The supporting detail, although accurate, is not relevant to the question.

Answer B

One way that nursing in 1860–75 was different from 1848–60 was that specialised training began to be offered in the years 1860–75. In the years 1848–60, nurses were not expected to have formal training but Nightingale set up a training school for nurses at St Thomas's Hospital, London in 1860. She also helped to set up a training school for midwives at King's College Hospital, London in 1861. This meant that training was very different in the later period.

Another difference in nursing was that in the years 1860–75, nurses played a more active role in the treatment of patients than they had done in the previous period. Florence Nightingale's Notes on Nursing, published in 1859, stressed the importance of careful observation of the patient and of keeping accurate records in order to be able to give a report to the doctor. This meant that nurses in 1860–75 were expected to monitor patients and report on their condition to the doctors. This was different from the previous situation, where they were simply caring for the patient, making sure they were clean and well-fed.

This is an excellent answer. Each paragraph begins by stating a difference and then provides supporting detail from each period to show what that difference was. It would be likely to receive full marks.

Challenge a friend

Use the Student Book to set a part (a) question for a friend. Then look at the answer. Does it do the following things?

☐ Identify two differences
☐ Provide supporting detail about each period to show what was different.

If it does, you can tell your friend that the answer is very good!

3. ACCELERATING CHANGE, 1875–1905

LEARNING OBJECTIVES

- Understand the importance of Koch's work in developing Pasteur's germ theory
- Analyse the impact of the work of Pasteur and Koch on surgery and public health
- Evaluate the role played by science in the development of medicine.

Pasteur had shown that microorganisms in the air cause decay but the link between microorganisms and disease had not yet been fully investigated. Therefore, until 1875, there had been little change in prevention or treatment of illness. However, in the period 1875–1905, both Pasteur and Koch produced vaccines that could prevent someone developing a disease.

In addition, by 1875, the link between hygiene and health had been recognised and the government now took responsibility for ensuring that housing and living conditions did not encourage the spread of disease. The Public Health Act 1875 covered a range of aspects that would help to keep people healthy and, unlike previous public health acts, this one was enforced.

Better understanding of bacteria and infection meant that standards in surgery improved. Antiseptic techniques became more widely accepted and aseptic techniques were developed. In addition, the discovery of blood groups meant that transfusion became possible. These developments made surgery safer and more complex operations became routine.

Work also began on developing new treatments. Ehrlich began to research treatment for syphilis and Marie Curie discovered that radiation could be used in medicine.

3.1 HOW DID KOCH DEVELOP PASTEUR'S WORK?

LEARNING OBJECTIVES

- Understand the key ideas of Pasteur's work and how they applied to medicine
- Analyse the role of Koch in developing Pasteur's work
- Evaluate the importance of the role of science.

Pasteur's ideas about microorganisms causing decay had become broadly accepted by 1875 but this had little impact on medicine. Even though Joseph Lister had shown that antiseptic techniques in surgery reduced the number of deaths from infection, the link to disease was not clear.

ROBERT KOCH

Robert Koch, a German doctor, was interested in Pasteur's ideas. Anthrax was a problem among the farm animals in the area where he lived and it was known that the disease could spread through infected blood. Koch wanted to prove scientifically that it was the anthrax microorganism which caused the disease. His wife bought him a microscope and, in 1872, he set up a small laboratory in his home; he published his work in 1876. He then carried out further research, developing methods of staining and photographing microorganisms. He also published work on bacterial infections of wounds in 1878.

EXTEND YOUR KNOWLEDGE

Pasteur named this technique 'vaccination' in honour of Edward Jenner's earlier work on smallpox in 1796. Jenner had found that giving someone the mild disease, cowpox, protected them against developing the killer disease, smallpox. He called his discovery vaccination because *vacca* is Latin for cow. However, this discovery only worked because there was a link between smallpox and cowpox; the technique could not be used against any other disease.

Koch's work was important for a number of reasons. Although he was a doctor, he did not focus on the symptoms of disease in humans. Instead, he investigated the microorganisms in laboratory tests. In his work, he showed that these techniques could be used to investigate a number of diseases and could lead to new ways of preventing disease. As a result, he was invited to move to Berlin; here, he received funding from the German government and developed a team of researchers.

PASTEUR AND CHICKEN CHOLERA

Meanwhile, Pasteur and his team had also been researching microorganisms. In 1878, Pasteur published his germ theory of infection, in which he linked disease to microorganisms.

Pasteur's team of scientists was studying chicken cholera by **injecting** chickens with a **culture** of the **bacteria**. When Pasteur's assistant went on holiday, a culture of the bacteria was left on one side and not used until a couple of weeks later. The chickens injected with this culture did not develop chicken cholera, so they were injected with a fresh culture. However, they still did not develop chicken cholera!

KEY TERMS

culture bacteria grown in controlled conditions, usually in a liquid or substance like agar jelly

vaccination the process of injecting weakened disease microorganisms in order to stimulate the body's defences and protect against the disease in future

Pasteur and his team realised that the first batch had been weakened by the delay in using it. Injecting this weakened version had stimulated the chicken's natural defences, so it was able to fight against the fresh culture when that was injected. This paved the way for further research to develop **vaccinations** against other diseases.

PASTEUR'S ANTHRAX VACCINE

SOURCE A

Pasteur and his assistant vaccinating a man against rabies.

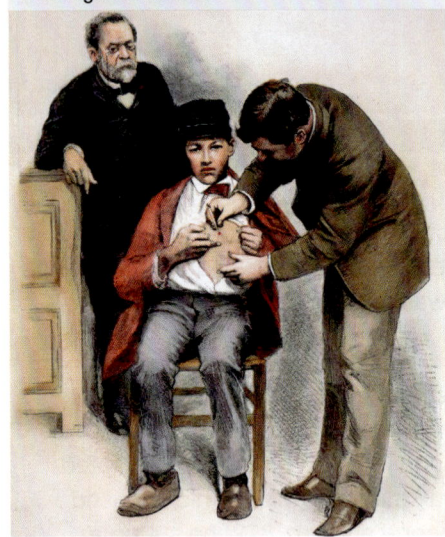

In 1881, Pasteur combined Koch's work with his own to prove that an anthrax vaccination could be used to protect sheep and cows. He publicly vaccinated 24 sheep, one goat and six cows while a control group of 24 sheep, one goat and four cows was not vaccinated. On 31 May, all the animals were inoculated with anthrax bacilli; 2 days later, the crowd reassembled. The vaccinated animals were all alive but in the control group, the goat and all the sheep were dead by the end of the day, and the four unprotected cows were swollen and feverish.

Pasteur wanted to investigate vaccines for human diseases but he could not carry out experiments on people. He began working on a vaccine against rabies, a disease which affects both animals and humans. Pasteur's vaccine was still at the experimental stage in 1885, when a 9-year-old boy, Joseph Meister, was brought to him after being bitten by a rabid dog. Normally, a vaccine cannot protect a person who already has the disease but rabies only develops once the microorganisms reach the brain. Knowing that the boy would die if he did nothing, Pasteur agreed to use his rabies vaccine and the boy's life was saved.

KOCH AND BACTERIOLOGY

Koch began to investigate different human diseases to see if he could identify specific microorganisms that caused particular diseases. He tested different microorganisms, seeing if they could be used to create a culture. He then injected these cultures into test animals to see whether the animals would develop particular diseases.

KEY TERM

Petri dish a small round, glass dish used in laboratory work

Using these methods, Koch and his team identified the microorganisms for tuberculosis in 1882 and cholera in 1883. Koch developed the use of agar jelly for growing cultures in a **Petri dish**. He also experimented with the use of industrial chemical dyes to stain microorganisms a different colour and make them easier to study under the microscope.

The study of bacteria developed and became a separate branch of science, called bacteriology. Koch has been called the 'father of bacteriology' because his methods and discoveries were the starting point for further discoveries. For example, the microorganisms responsible for deadly diseases such as tetanus, pneumonia, meningitis, diphtheria and dysentery were all identified during the 1880s and 1890s.

PASTEUR AND KOCH

In some ways, Pasteur and Koch were rivals because they both wanted to make significant scientific discoveries. Their rivalry was increased by the hostility between their countries, particularly in 1870–71, when France and Germany were at war. The French and German governments were each keen to gain honour from the work of their scientists, so they provided funding for the research teams and equipment.

However, although Pasteur and Koch did not work together, their research was published in scientific journals and at conferences. This meant that they knew about each other's work and could build on it.

ACCELERATING CHANGE, 1875–1905 — CHANGES IN MEDICINE, c1848–c1948

Other scientists could also read about their work but it was some time before many of these new developments were accepted in medicine. The attitude of doubtful scientists and doctors meant that the public knew almost nothing about the work of Pasteur and Koch – especially since it took time to develop each vaccine and it was even longer before any new treatment was developed.

SOURCE B

A cartoon from 1880, showing Robert Koch killing tuberculosis. His saddle is labelled 'Investigation' and his weapon is a microscope; tuberculosis is shown as a snake. The caption compares Koch to St George killing a dragon.

▼ The work of Pasteur and Koch

PASTEUR	DATE	KOCH
Published experiments on the germ theory	1861	
Research proved that silkworms were killed by microorganisms	1865–70	
	1875	Identified anthrax microorganism
Published germ theory of infection, which linked microorganisms to disease	1878	
Developed a way of creating a vaccine to protect against chicken cholera	1879	
Developed a vaccine against anthrax in sheep and cows	1881	
	1882	Identified the tuberculosis microorganism
	1883	Identified the cholera microorganism
Used the rabies vaccine on a human for the first time	1885	

ACTIVITY

1 Explain how Pasteur's work led to the development of vaccinations.
2 Explain how Koch's work in identifying different microorganisms contributed to the development of vaccinations.
3 Why was Koch regarded as the 'father of bacteriology'?
4 Copy the table above and add an extra column, with the heading 'Factors'. In this column, say whether each development was helped by the factors of technology, communication and government.

EXAM-STYLE QUESTION

AO1 AO2

SKILLS: PROBLEM SOLVING, REASONING, DECISION MAKING

How far did understanding of disease change in the years 1848–90?

You may use the following in your answer:
- four humours
- Pasteur's germ theory of infection.

You **must** also use information of your own.

(16 marks)

HINT

In order to show change, you need to explain what people thought caused disease in 1848 and compare this with what they thought by 1890. However, this question asks 'how far' that understanding changed. This means that you should also be looking for some examples of continuity. You can then weigh the two sides of the issue in order to decide how much actually changed.

3.2 HOW DID SURGERY IMPROVE?

LEARNING OBJECTIVES

- Understand the move from antiseptic surgery to aseptic surgery
- Analyse the factors affecting developments in surgery
- Evaluate the progress made in surgery by 1905.

THE IMPACT OF LISTER'S ANTISEPTIC TECHNIQUES

Lister had introduced antiseptic techniques in surgery but many doctors had not been convinced by his ideas and not everyone believed in microorganisms.

In 1877, Lister became Professor of Surgery at King's College Hospital, London. The germ theory and Lister's antiseptic techniques were slowly becoming accepted, especially after Robert Koch identified the microorganism causing blood poisoning in 1878. However, there was still resistance because Lister's carbolic spray made operations difficult.

It was therefore a huge improvement when Koch developed a steam steriliser in 1878. Pasteur had shown that microorganisms could be killed by heat so Koch developed the idea to use heat to **sterilise** equipment and dressings.

EXTRACT A

A modern historian describes opposition to Lister's ideas.

Many of Lister's colleagues laughed at him, and Hughes Bennett, a professor of medicine in Edinburgh, asked scornfully, 'Where are these little beasts? Show them to us and we shall believe in them. Has anyone seen them yet?' But Lister never bothered to reply and it is said that he only heaved an occasional sigh at the world's stupidity.

SOURCE C

A steam steriliser, which could be used to sterilise surgical instruments.

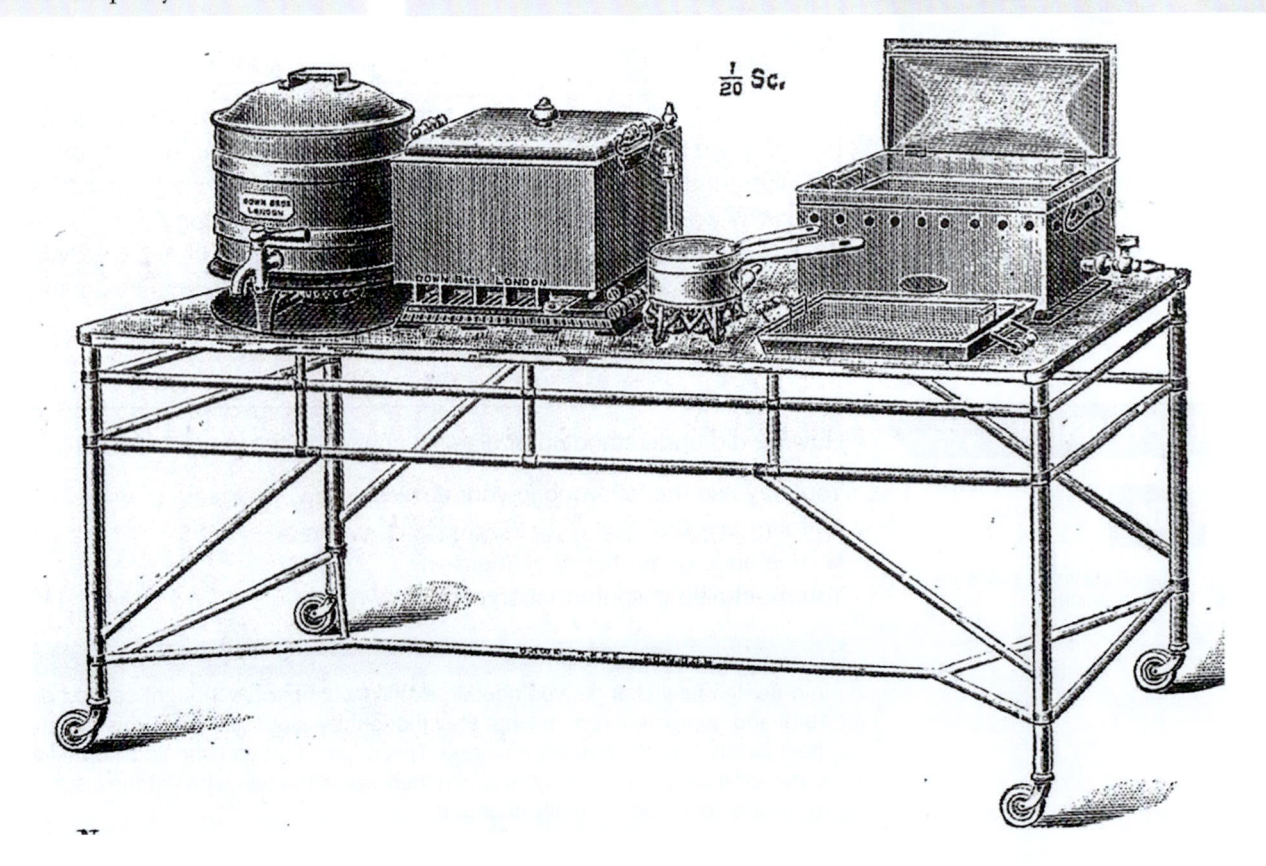

ACCELERATING CHANGE, 1875–1905   CHANGES IN MEDICINE, c1848–c1948

SOURCE D

A painting showing Lister and Pasteur meeting in France, 1892. Lister is walking up the steps and Pasteur is on the stage; he is old and being supported by the president of France.

ASEPTIC SURGERY

KEY TERM

aseptic techniques methods used to try to prevent microorganisms from coming into contact with the open wound during an operation

As the understanding of microorganisms increased, new techniques were introduced. These techniques aimed to do more than simply fight infections (antiseptic surgery); now, surgeons tried to prevent microorganisms getting anywhere near the open wound and creating infection (**aseptic** surgery). This went beyond killing the microorganisms on the equipment and around the wound. Now, operations were carried out in clean operating theatres without spectators. In addition, surgeons wore clean clothes, put masks over their mouths and wore rubber gloves to prevent microorganisms entering the wound.

EXTEND YOUR KNOWLEDGE

In 1890, Dr Halstead asked Goodyear Rubber Company to make some gloves for his nurse, Caroline Hampton, because carbolic acid severely affected the eczema on her hands. Surgeons then also began to wear rubber gloves as this was another way to reduce infection.

BLOOD LOSS

Blood loss was always a problem in surgery. Even when the problems of pain and infection had been solved, operations had to be completed quickly, before the patient lost too much blood. As well as his work on antiseptic techniques, Lister had been experimenting with ways to reduce the loss of blood. During an operation, pressure was usually placed on an artery to stop the flow of blood. Afterwards, any **blood vessels** which had been cut were sealed. This was usually done by cauterisation, an extremely painful process which involved placing a piece of hot iron against the blood vessel and sealing the ends by heat.

Sometimes, the end of the blood vessel was tied with threads called ligatures. However, ligatures could become hard and prevent the wound healing properly, or they could be a new source of infection. Lister had experimented with silk ligatures soaked in carbolic acid but these were not always effective.

In 1881, Lister published the results of his work using **catgut** as ligatures. Catgut could be soaked in carbolic acid, so it did not create infection in the wound. Better still, it **dissolved** in the body after 2 to 3 weeks, so catgut ligatures did not prevent the body healing properly.

> **KEY TERM**
>
> **catgut** despite the name, catgut is made from sheep's intestines, which are emptied and used like threads or thin fibres; because it comes from an animal, it is less likely to cause problems inside a body

> **SOURCE E**
>
> An account of Lister's work on ligatures, written by one of his colleagues in 1926.
>
> After developing antiseptic techniques, Lister searched for a satisfactory ligature. Silk had been used previously, unsterilised of course, but it led to pus in the wound and death from infection. Silver wire was tried and irritated the wound less but it could not be absorbed by the body. Lister wanted to find a material that would be accepted by the body's tissues and he thought that using some animal substance would be less likely to be rejected. Tendons seemed a suitable material and kangaroo tendon in particular; why kangaroo we did not know, except that it was longer than that of other animals.
>
> Lister tried it first upon a horse, using antiseptic procedures, and the wound healed well. However, kangaroo tendon was difficult to obtain so he tried catgut instead.

PAIN RELIEF: COCAINE

Although chloroform appeared to cause fewer problems than ether, there were a number of sudden deaths during operations using chloroform. Scientists continued to search for a better anaesthetic. **Cocaine** was used but it was not very suitable as it was **addictive**. However, in 1884, it was found that cocaine could be used as a local anaesthetic, just numbing (causing a loss of feeling in) a part of the body. (The alternative was a general anaesthetic, which made the patient unconscious.) A safer version, called novocaine, was developed in 1905.

These improved conditions and techniques made surgery safer for patients and meant that surgeons were able to carry out more complicated operations. King Edward VII's coronation in 1902 had to be postponed because he had **appendicitis** and needed an operation. Luckily, the surgeon was experienced and had carried out this operation over 1,000 times before.

ACCELERATING CHANGE, 1875–1905   CHANGES IN MEDICINE, c1848–c1948

ACTIVITY

1 Lister was the first doctor to be knighted. Why was his contribution to surgery so important?
2 Explain why aseptic surgery was better than antiseptic surgery.
3 Which factor had most impact on surgery in the years 1875–1905: scientific knowledge or technological developments?
4 What problems of surgery remained to be solved?

Surgeon is wearing a clean gown over his clothes and a cap on his head to prevent germs transferring to the wound

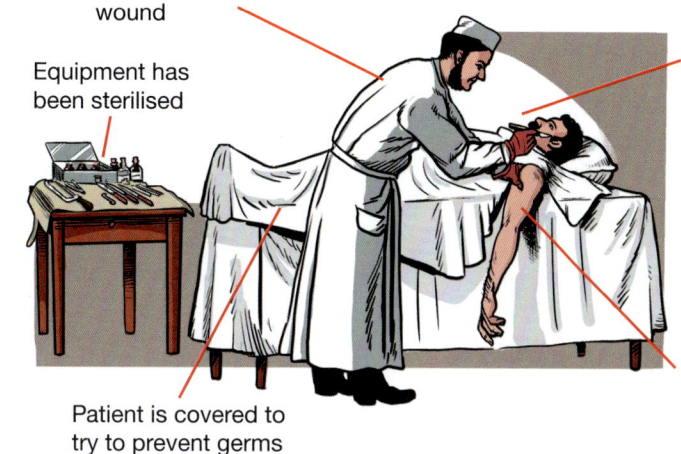

Surgeon is wearing rubber gloves to prevent infection inside the wound

Equipment has been sterilised

Local anaesthetic – patient remains conscious but pain in the arm is not felt

Patient is covered to try to prevent germs getting into the wound

▲ Figure 3.1 How far had the problems of surgery been solved?

EXAM-STYLE QUESTION

AO1 **AO2**

SKILLS ADAPTIVE LEARNING

Explain **two** causes of improvements in surgery in the years 1848–1905.

(8 marks)

HINT

For each of the examples you include in your answer, you need to identify a cause of improvement (for example, a person's work, a key event or a factor such as science or technology). You need to explain how each of the causes you identify is linked to a specific improvement in surgery.

3.3 WHAT WAS THE IMPACT OF THE PUBLIC HEALTH ACT 1875?

LEARNING OBJECTIVES

- Understand the terms of the Public Health Act 1875
- Analyse the factors involved in change
- Evaluate the impact of the Public Health Act 1875.

The 1866 Sanitary Act had made local authorities responsible for sewers, water and street cleaning. The 1875 Public Health Act went further, making local councils responsible for a range of public health measures which had a huge impact on hygiene and housing (see pages 32–33).

Local councils could charge taxes to pay for these improvements but the improvements had to be carried out. However, this was not an easy task. For example, digging tunnels for piped water or for sewers needed a large workforce and appropriate technology. Bazalgette's sewer system for London involved nearly 21,000 km of sewers feeding into six interceptor sewers; the work on just these six interceptor sewers meant excavating 2.7 million cubic metres of earth and used over 300 million bricks and 670,000 cubic metres of concrete and Portland cement. Portland cement is a very strong version of concrete but the mixture needs to be heated to over 1,000 degrees Celsius.

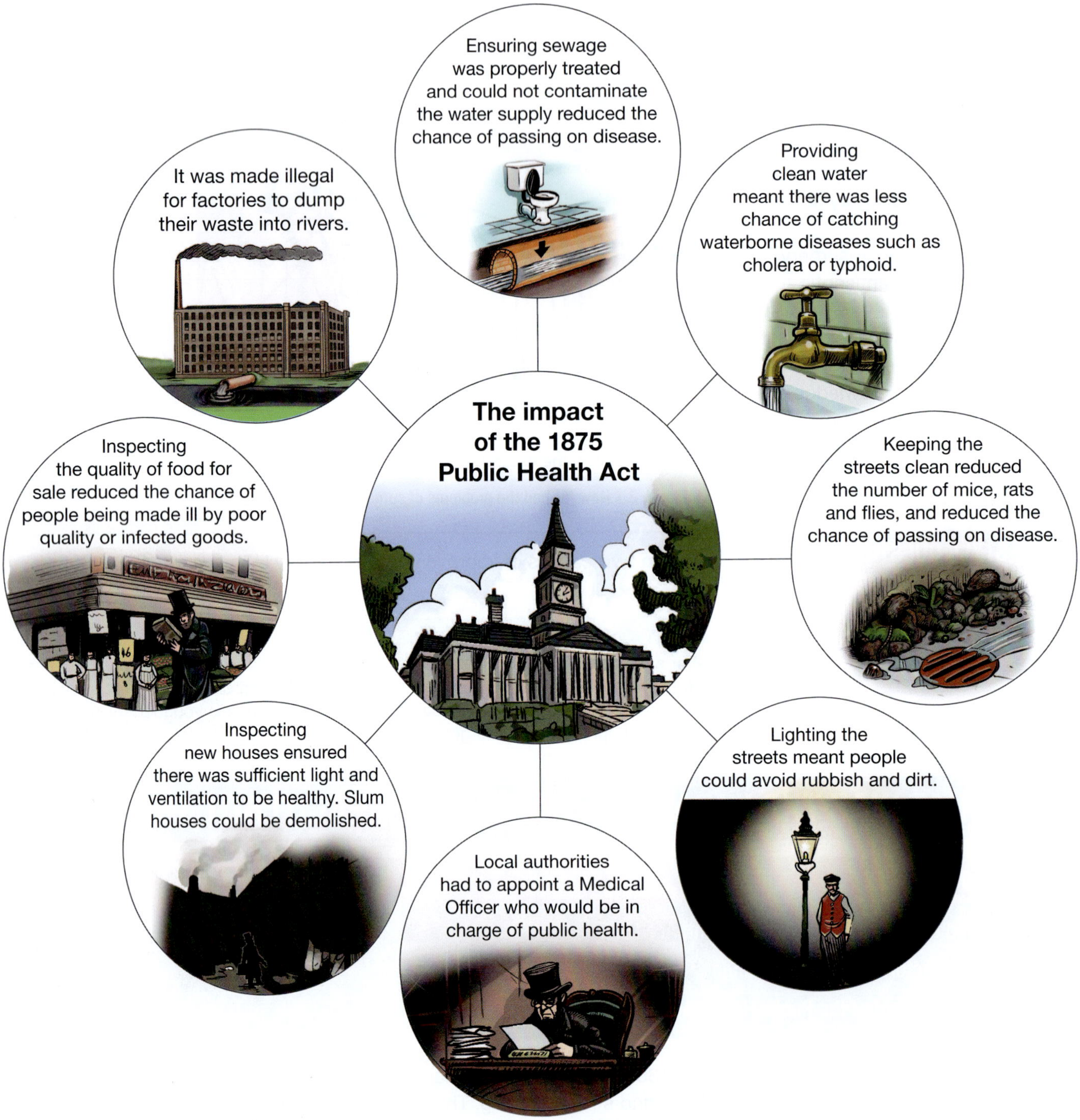

ACCELERATING CHANGE, 1875–1905 CHANGES IN MEDICINE, c1848–c1948

The impact of the 1875 Public Health Act

- Ensuring sewage was properly treated and could not contaminate the water supply reduced the chance of passing on disease.
- Providing clean water meant there was less chance of catching waterborne diseases such as cholera or typhoid.
- It was made illegal for factories to dump their waste into rivers.
- Keeping the streets clean reduced the number of mice, rats and flies, and reduced the chance of passing on disease.
- Inspecting the quality of food for sale reduced the chance of people being made ill by poor quality or infected goods.
- Lighting the streets meant people could avoid rubbish and dirt.
- Inspecting new houses ensured there was sufficient light and ventilation to be healthy. Slum houses could be demolished.
- Local authorities had to appoint a Medical Officer who would be in charge of public health.

▲ Figure 3.2 The impact of the 1875 Public Health Act

Other examples of technology's role in improving public health are the use of pipes for water supplies and gas lighting and also Bazalgette's use of steam powered engines in his pumping stations.

Other acts of parliament were also passed that improved the health of the public.
- In 1875, the Artisans' Dwellings Act gave local authorities the power to buy and demolish slum housing.
- The Food and Drugs Act 1875 tried to improve the standard of food being sold. At this point, many dangerous practices were common, for example,

ACCELERATING CHANGE, 1875–1905 | CHANGES IN MEDICINE, c1848–c1948

butchers would often paint meat red so that it appeared fresh; shopkeepers might mix sand with flour to make it weigh more when it was sold; and tea leaves were dried, dyed and sold again. Sometimes, the things added to make food weigh more or look fresh were poisonous, such as lead or strychnine.

- The 1876 River Pollution Prevention Act made it illegal for factories to put their waste, including chemicals, into rivers.
- The 1889 Infectious Disease (Notification) Act ordered householders or doctors in London to report any cases of infectious disease to the local Medical Health Officer. This law was extended to the rest of the country in 1899. This also led to new **isolation hospitals** being built.

The Park Hospital in London was opened in 1897. This was one of five new hospitals built to cope with cases of infectious disease in London. It had 48 wards for up to 368 patients with **scarlet fever**, and 24 wards for up to 120 patients with **diptheria** and fever. There were also isolation wards where there was a large distance between patients.

SOURCE F
The ward for patients with tuberculosis c1908.

FACTORS AFFECTING PUBLIC HEALTH

The government had a major impact on public health in the years 1875–1905 because it passed a number of laws which made changes in hygiene and living standards. Local authorities were usually responsible for implementing these laws and acted on a range of issues.

This reflects changing attitudes towards the role of government. Equally, as more people were allowed to vote in elections, governments began to do more to win the support of ordinary people.

However, the role of science and technology was crucial. New understanding about microorganisms and how diseases spread showed the importance of improved hygiene. New technology made piped water and sewer systems possible.

New understanding about disease also showed that it was necessary to isolate patients with infectious diseases, and highlighted the importance of the authorities to co-ordinate action.

ACTIVITY

1. What was the role of local authorities in making improvements in each of these areas?
   - housing
   - sanitation
   - dealing with outbreaks of infectious disease.
2. How important was the role of central government in these improvements?

EXAM-STYLE QUESTION

AO1 AO2

SKILLS PROBLEM SOLVING, REASONING, DECISION MAKING

How far did public health provision change in the years 1848–1905?

You may use the following in your answer:
- cholera epidemics
- Public Health Act 1875.

You **must** also use information of your own. **(16 marks)**

HINT

The question says 'how far'. This means you need to weigh areas where there was change against areas where there was no change. Alternatively, you could compare the early part of the period with the later part; there were very limited improvements from 1848 to 1875 but quite a lot of improvements from 1875 to 1905.

The two stimulus points in the question suggest different aspects that you could include in your answer but you need to think of a third aspect to include as well.

3.4 HOW DID SCIENCE LEAD TO RAPID CHANGE IN MEDICINE?

LEARNING OBJECTIVES

- Understand the scientific developments that affected medicine
- Analyse the impact of scientific discoveries
- Evaluate the importance of key individuals.

BLOOD TRANSFUSIONS

Attempts to carry out blood **transfusions** in the past had often caused the death of the patient but no one understood why. However, in 1901, an Austrian doctor called Karl Landsteiner discovered that there were different **blood types**: A, B and O; in 1902, he identified a fourth type, AB. Doctors realised that patients could die if they were given blood of a different type – for example, if a person with type A blood was given type B blood. (In 1907, it was discovered that type O blood could be given safely to anyone, whatever their blood group. The reasons for this were not fully understood.)

Transfusions could now be carried out successfully, as long as the patient was given blood from the right group. This would have a huge impact on surgery

ACCELERATING CHANGE, 1875–1905 — CHANGES IN MEDICINE, c1848–c1948

and would also help people who had blood disorders such as **anaemia** and **leukaemia**, liver problems or **jaundice**.

The main problem now was that the blood **donor** had to be present in order for the transfusion to be carried out and it was not always possible to find a donor of the right blood group. Furthermore, blood starts to **clot** as soon as it leaves the body so the tubes used in transfusion could also become blocked. The improvement in scientific knowledge about blood groups was important but progress in surgery could not really happen until scientific knowledge had developed ways to prevent blood clotting and technology had overcome the problems of storing blood and the process of transfusion.

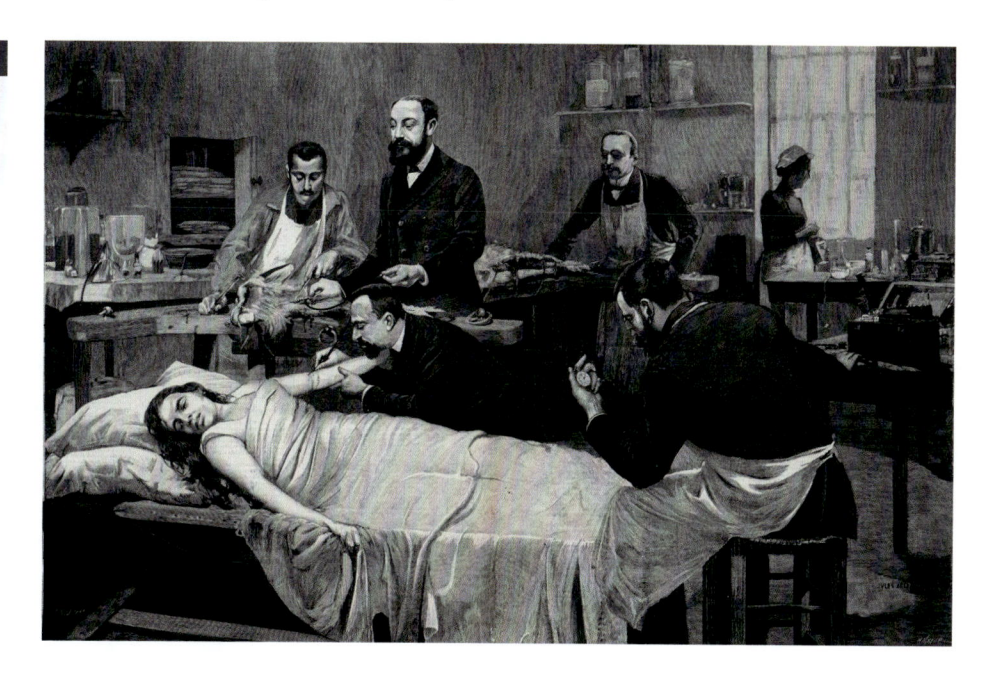

KEY TERMS

anaemia a condition where the patient is constantly tired because the blood does not have enough red blood cells to carry oxygen around the body

jaundice a condition where the skin and the eyes look yellow because the body cannot deal with old red blood cells properly

SOURCE G

A photograph from the late 19th century showing a blood transfusion where the donor is present.

IMPROVEMENTS IN SCIENTIFIC KNOWLEDGE

The work of Pasteur and Koch led to rapid changes in scientific knowledge. In particular, Koch's use of agar jelly to grow cultures of bacteria, and his use of chemical dyes to stain bacteria, made it much easier to study microorganisms. Koch had found that certain dyes were taken up by specific microorganisms; this made it easier to see the microorganisms when studying the cells under a microscope. However, although this work had helped scientists and doctors to understand the cause of various diseases, and even to develop vaccinations to prevent people catching some diseases, no new treatments were available yet.

Diphtheria is caused by microorganisms in milk. Nowadays, these microorganisms are killed when the milk is **pasteurised**. In the 19th century, however, diphtheria killed approximately 8,000 children each year. A Russian scientist called Metchnikoff showed that the diphtheria microorganism generated a poison in the body; this poison created a **membrane** in the throat which gradually stopped the patient breathing.

KEY TERM

antitoxins some microorganisms invade cells in the body and release poison or toxins; white blood cells produce antibodies to fight the microorganisms causing disease; antitoxins are types of antibodies which neutralise those toxins and stop them from having an effect

In 1890, Emil von Behring identified the **antitoxins** produced by the body to fight diphtheria. He then found that if he injected these antitoxins into a patient, the patient's body was more able to fight the disease. He could cure diphtheria!

PAUL EHRLICH AND THE FIRST MAGIC BULLET

KEY TERM

magic bullet a treatment that would kill the disease-carrying microorgansims without affecting other cells in the body

Paul Ehrlich had been a member of Koch's team and had also worked with Behring. In 1896, he became the leader of his own team as he wanted to research possible treatments. He had worked on Koch's discovery that certain chemicals would only dye specific microorganisms, without affecting other microorganisms. He also knew from Behring's work that antitoxins would only attack specific microorganisms. He wondered if these ideas could be combined: a chemical could be linked to something that would kill the microorganisms causing a specific disease. If this worked, those microorganisms could be killed without harming any others – the treatment would be a '**magic bullet**' that killed the disease but did no other harm.

If left untreated, the disease **syphilis** affects the brain and can lead to a **stroke**, dementia, vision problems and heart problems. Because of these symptoms, syphilis was greatly feared. However, the remedy that was used was equally dangerous, because it involved mercury (a poisonous metal which caused kidney failure).

In 1905, Ehrlich began experimenting to see if he could find a 'magic bullet' that would treat syphilis without affecting other cells in the body. He tried various **compounds** based on different strengths of the poison arsenic. In 1909, after 606 different compounds had been tried, the first magic bullet was found. It was given the name Salvarsan 606 and it was the first chemical cure for a disease.

SOURCE H

A German banknote, showing Ehrlich and a microscope.

EXTEND YOUR KNOWLEDGE

The discovery of Salvarsan 606 almost didn't happen. In 1909, Dr Sahachiro Hata joined the research team and reviewed some previous experiments. He found that compound 606 had been wrongly reported as ineffective in 1907; the team had carried on searching for a magic bullet without realising they had already found it.

ACCELERATING CHANGE, 1875–1905   **CHANGES IN MEDICINE, c1848–c1948**   59

THE DEVELOPMENT OF X-RAYS

As new areas of science developed, supported by new technology, the discovery of **X-rays** had a major impact on medicine.

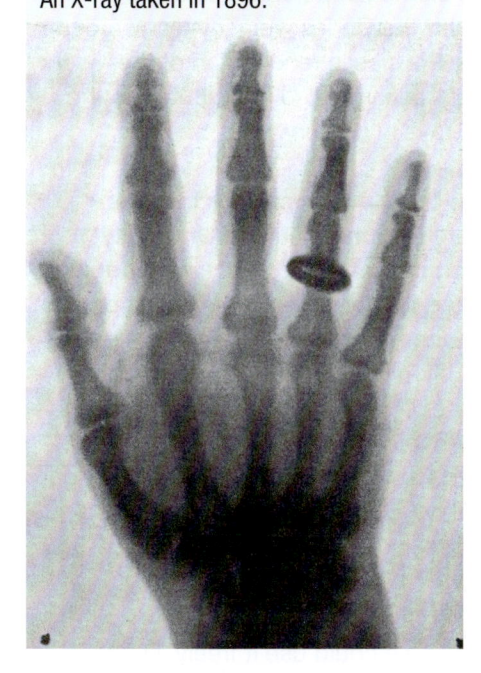

In 1895, a German physicist called Wilhelm Röntgen was studying cathode rays, where a glass tube contains gases at low pressure and an electric current is passed through them. The tube was covered in black cardboard and the room was darkened. However, there was a bright glow where minerals on another piece of cardboard had begun to shine.

Röntgen experimented with different thicknesses of paper around the tube and found varying levels of light were recorded on photographic plates on the other side of the room. He realised that, while normal rays of light could not pass through the black card around the tube, these unknown rays could; he called them X-rays.

X-RAYS AND MEDICINE

When his wife placed her hand between the cathode ray tube and the photographic plate, Röntgen found that the photographic plate showed an image of her hand, with the bones and her wedding ring showing clearly.

Röntgen published his findings in December 1895 but he did not take out a **patent** (which would have given him legal rights over his discovery); this was so that other people could use it freely. As early as 1896, many hospitals, including the London Royal Hospital, had an X-ray machine installed.

SOURCE I
An X-ray taken in 1896.

KEY TERM

patent this is like copyright or a trademark, the product is owned by the person taking out the patent, and anyone who uses it must pay the owner

X-rays could be used to show the details of broken bones so that the break could be set properly. This is important because if broken bones are not set in the right position, the person may end up walking with a limp, or with reduced movement in a limb. The value of X-rays in surgery was also obvious, particularly in times of war. An X-ray could show exactly where a bullet was, which meant the surgeon spent less time searching inside a wound. This reduced the chances of infection or further damage to blood vessels. Similarly, when a soldier was injured by **shrapnel**, the surgeon could make sure he had removed every bit from his body.

Doctors also found X-rays useful in diagnosing other problems. For example, the disease **tuberculosis** showed up as a shadow on the lungs if the patient was X-rayed, and bone tumours could also be seen. It was also possible to study a patient's internal organs if the patient was given something to drink that would show up on an X-ray as it travelled through the body.

EXAM-STYLE QUESTION

AO1   **AO2**

SKILLS   PROBLEM SOLVING, REASONING, DECISION MAKING

How far did scientific knowledge lead to changes in medicine in the years 1860–1905?

You may use the following in your answer:
- Pasteur's germ theory
- blood groups.

You **must** also use information of your own.   **(16 marks)**

HINT

You need to show ways in which scientific knowledge led to changes in medicine. You should also look at examples where new scientific knowledge did not have an immediate effect on medicine. You should then weigh the evidence on both sides in order to reach a judgement.

HOW MUCH IMPACT DID MARIE CURIE HAVE ON MEDICINE?

Marie Sklodowska was a Polish chemist who came to Paris in 1891. Here, she met and married a French physicist called Pierre Curie. In 1896, Henri Becquerel discovered radioactivity and Marie and Pierre Curie began to work together on radioactive material. In 1898, they announced the discovery of two new scientific elements: polonium and radium. In 1903, Becquerel and the Curies were jointly awarded the Nobel Prize for Physics in recognition of their work on **radiation**. Their research also contributed to the development of X-rays in surgery.

Pierre died in 1906 but Marie Curie took over his position in a research laboratory at the University of Paris and continued the work. In 1910, a new Radium Institute was created for her, where she could continue her research on radium. She led the research into using radioactivity to shrink or kill tumours. At first, radium was placed as close to the tumour as possible; then radium was inserted into the tumour itself. This was the basis of radiotherapy which is still used in the fight against cancer today (although the technique used now is safer and the dose is carefully measured).

Like Röntgen, Marie Curie did not patent her work. This meant other people could use it freely. Doctors experimented with the use of radioactivity; for example, testing it as a treatment for **epilepsy** and **acne**. Dangerous side effects were noted, but its benefits in cancer cases were clear. The importance of Curie's work was recognised when she was awarded a second Nobel Prize in 1911, this time for chemistry.

SOURCE J
Marie Curie in her laboratory.

EXTEND YOUR KNOWLEDGE

Marie Curie was the first woman to receive a Nobel Prize and, at the time of writing, she is one of only two people to receive a Nobel Prize in two different fields. Curie died at the age of 67, due to leukaemia; we now know this illness was caused by radiation.

MARIE CURIE AND MOBILE X-RAYS

During the First World War (1914–18), Marie Curie used her own money to help to equip ambulances with X-ray equipment; she even drove these ambulances to the front lines herself. These mobile X-ray units became known as '*les petites Curies*' ('the little Curies') and they meant that injured soldiers could be X-rayed and operated on as soon as possible. The International Red Cross made Curie head of its Radiological Service and she ran training courses to teach medical assistants and doctors about the new techniques.

ACCELERATING CHANGE

The work of Pasteur and Koch was a huge breakthrough in improving understanding of disease. This provided the basis for developments in both prevention and treatment. However, doctors and scientists were slow to accept the new ideas and it was a long time before there were significant changes in prevention and treatment. Nevertheless, Pasteur and Koch had a major impact on public health and surgery.

Research teams and government funding were important in the large-scale testing methods being used at this time. Meanwhile, changes in technology helped scientific investigations; for example, more powerful microscopes, the **hypodermic needle** and X-ray machines. In addition, the science of bacteriology developed, helped by chemistry.

ACTIVITY

1 Write a list of the scientific discoveries made during this period. Then arrange them in order of importance.
2 With a partner, discuss which piece of technology was most important in this period.
3 In small groups, debate the importance of Koch, Ehrlich and Curie. Who made the most important contribution to medicine?
4 Explain how one development can be a starting point for another. For example, could Ehrlich have found Salvarsan 606 without the work of Koch and Behring?
5 Why did change happen so quickly in this period, when it had taken so long for Pasteur's ideas to be accepted?

Factor	Public health	Surgery	Prevention and treatment
Scientific knowledge – the impact of Pasteur's germ theory and the work of Pasteur and Koch on microorganisms	Better understanding of how infectious diseases spread and the need for improvements in hygiene and living conditions Public Health Act 1875 gathered existing legislation and actions by local authorities into an overall national standard	Better understanding of infection and the development of antiseptic and aseptic techniques	Better understanding of the cause of illness, leading to the development of vaccinations and research for treatment for some illnesses The development of bacteriology as a new branch of medicine
Scientific knowledge – blood groups		The identification of blood groups made transfusions possible if a suitable donor was present	Blood transfusions could help with some illnesses, however, scientific knowledge about how to stop blood clotting was needed before blood could be stored
Scientific methods			Research began to involve large-scale testing methods
Technology – X-rays		X-rays could help locate foreign objects in a wound or a break in a bone	X-rays could help in diagnosis and treatment of some diseases
Technology – improved microscopes			More powerful microscopes allowed more detailed research
Technology – chemical dyes			Being able to stain microorganisms meant they could be studied more easily under a microscope
Technology – hypodermic needle		Hypodermic needles helped to control the amount of blood being used in transfusions	Being able to measure amounts of blood or to inject precise amounts was important in research, blood transfusions and vaccinations
Government	Parliament passed laws forcing local authorities to take action to improve public health		Government provided some funding for research projects
Attitudes	People became more willing to accept the role of government in public health	Doctors became more willing to accept antiseptic and aseptic techniques	People became more willing to accept vaccinations

▲ Figure 3.3 Factors affecting medicine

RECAP

RECALL QUIZ

1. Explain why Koch has been called the 'father of bacteriology'.
2. What is a vaccination?
3. Name three techniques of aseptic surgery.
4. What is a ligature?
5. Give three examples of changes made by the Public Health Act 1875.
6. Why was the discovery of blood groups important?
7. What was a 'magic bullet'?
8. What are X-rays?
9. How are X-rays used in medicine?
10. Why was the study of radiation important in medicine?

CHECKPOINT

STRENGTHEN

S1 Explain why Koch's work on identifying microorganisms was important for medicine.
S2 Explain why the Public Health Act 1875 was important in improving the overall health of the nation.
S3 Explain why Marie Curie's work in physics and chemistry had an impact on medicine.

CHALLENGE

C1 Why did it take so long after the work of Pasteur and Koch for new treatments to be developed?
C2 Was science or technology more important in improving medicine in the years 1870–1905?
C3 Were the greatest advances in the years 1870–1905 in medicine, surgery or public health?

SUMMARY

- There was now a much clearer understanding of the cause of disease and vaccinations for different diseases began to be created.
- Progress in treatment was still slow because scientists had to study the bacteria causing each disease before they could work on a cure.
- Research now involved large-scale testing and the role of research teams and government funding became more important.
- Developments in technology helped to improve research, diagnosis and treatment.
- Surgery became much safer as aseptic techniques began to be used.
- The government took responsibility for enforcing better standards of public health.
- The discovery of blood groups made transfusions possible but the donor had to be present.
- Ehrlich was working on the first 'magic bullet', which would kill the bacteria causing disease without harming the rest of the body.
- X-rays were discovered and could be used to help surgery.
- Marie Curie showed that radiation could also be used in medicine.

ACCELERATING CHANGE, 1875–1905 — CHANGES IN MEDICINE, c1848–c1948

EXAM GUIDANCE: PART (C) QUESTIONS

A01 **A02**

SKILLS PROBLEM SOLVING, REASONING, DECISION MAKING

Question to be answered: How far was Lister responsible for the improvements in surgery in the years 1860–1905?

You may use the following in your answer:
- carbolic spray
- X-rays.

You must also use information of your own. **(16 marks)**

1 **Analysis Question 1: What is the question type testing?**
In this question, you have to demonstrate that you have knowledge and understanding of the key features and characteristics of the period studied. In this particular case, you need to show your knowledge and understanding of improvements in surgery in the years 1860–1905 and how Lister's work influenced these improvements.

You also have to explain, analyse and make judgements about historical events and periods; here, you need to give an explanation and reach a judgement about the role of various factors in bringing about changes.

2 **Analysis Question 2: What do I have to do to answer the question well?**
- You have been given two topics on which to write. You don't have to use them and can provide your own topics. (But it seems sensible to do so!)
- You must not simply give information. Think about what improvements these developments caused.
- You are also asked 'how far' Lister was responsible for the improvements in surgery. When discussing these developments, you need to consider whether Lister's work caused each change. The stimulus points for a question like this will usually include one hint that supports the statement and one hint that suggests an alternative.
- The question says you must use information of your own. You should include at least one extra factor, beyond the two topics you have been given. For example, you could talk about the development of aseptic surgery. Alternatively, you could say that Lister's work depended on Pasteur's germ theory and, in fact, Pasteur should get credit for the improvements.

3 **Analysis Question 3: Are there any techniques I can use to make it very clear that I am doing what is needed to be successful?**
This is a 16-mark question and you need to make sure you give a substantial answer. You will be working against the clock so you may wish to use the following techniques to help you succeed.
- Don't write a lengthy introduction. Give a brief introduction which answers the question immediately and shows what your paragraphs are going to be about.
- Make sure you stay focused and avoid just writing narrative. To help with this, try to use the words of the question at the beginning of each paragraph.
- Remember this question asks about causation. As with question (b), you must make sure your answer explains why each point means that Lister was (or was not) responsible for the improvements in surgery.

64 ACCELERATING CHANGE, 1875–1905   CHANGES IN MEDICINE, c1848–c1948

Good introduction

Answer
The period 1860–1905 was one where there were some major developments in surgery which greatly improved the survival rate. The use of anaesthetics had actually increased the death rate because they hadn't solved the problem of infection, so Lister's work developing antiseptic techniques in the 1860s was a major improvement. However, to some extent, Lister's work was based on Pasteur's germ theory and later developments were based on new technology, so Lister cannot be given all the credit for the improvements.

Nice paragraph. Answers the question, gives contextual knowledge and links improvements in surgery to the work of Lister.

Lister read about Pasteur's germ theory and made the link to infection in surgery. He also knew about the use of carbolic acid to deal with sewage and experimented with the use of carbolic acid to fight infection in surgery. He developed antiseptic techniques to keep the instruments clean, to spray the wound and the surgeon's hands while operating, and to keep the bandages clean. As a result, deaths from infection were dramatically reduced. Even though his work depended on Pasteur's germ theory, it was Lister who made the connection to surgery and Lister who experimented and publicised antiseptic techniques, so he deserves the credit for the development of antiseptic surgery.

This is good detail, but you only imply that these developments have nothing to do with Lister. You need to explicitly link the information here to the question about how far Lister was responsible for improvements in surgery.

There were many developments in surgery in the period 1875–1905. New techniques were developed to sterilise the instruments by using steam and the surgeon wore gloves and a face mask to prevent any microorganisms being transferred during the operation. There was also new technology such as X-rays which helped surgeons by showing where bones were broken or if something was inside the wound.

This is a very disappointing paragraph. Landsteiner's discovery did not have much impact on surgery within the timescale of the question. In addition, the answer does not link this to the question, it's just a statement that is vaguely about surgery.

There were also developments in blood transfusions because Landsteiner showed there were different blood groups in 1901. People realised that the blood group had to be matched to make transfusions work.

Good concise finish; this makes a clear judgement about how far Lister was responsible for the improvements in surgery.

Although Lister could not have developed antiseptic techniques without Pasteur's work, Lister does deserve credit for many improvements in surgery in the 1860s and 1870s. The later improvements, such as aseptic surgery, built on his work. However, he cannot be given credit for all the improvements in surgery because new technology such as X-rays had nothing to do with Lister.

What are the strengths and weaknesses of this answer?
The teacher comments show strengths and weaknesses. Notice that the weaker second half of the answer has lots of detail but this is not used to answer the question. If there had been three paragraphs like the one on Lister and antiseptic techniques, this would have been a very good answer.

Work with a friend
Discuss with a friend how you would rewrite the weaker paragraphs in this answer so that the whole answer could get very high marks.

Challenge a friend
Use the Student Book to set a similar part (c) question for a friend. Then look at the answer. Does it do the following things?

☐ Identify improvements
☐ Provide detailed information about the improvements
☐ Show how the stated factor was responsible for the improvements
☐ Consider examples that challenge the statement
☐ Provide a factor other than the two given in the question
☐ Address 'how far?'

4. GOVERNMENT ACTION AND WAR, 1905–20

LEARNING OBJECTIVES

- Understand the impact on public health of the reforms introduced by the Liberal governments
- Understand the impact on medicine and surgery of the First World War
- Evaluate improvements in public health, medicine and surgery.

The early 20th century was a time when two factors had a major impact on medicine.

The role of government in public health had developed during the late 19th century. Now, it was to expand far beyond issues of hygiene and housing. A key period was 1906–11; during this time, a series of laws was passed. These laws aimed to improve the health of the nation by providing medical checks and support for people at risk of ill health.

Shortly afterwards, the First World War led to injuries on a far greater scale than any previous war. This placed pressure on doctors and scientists to develop new methods of treatment and new techniques in surgery. The war also increased demand for nurses and doctors and allowed women to become more involved in medicine.

4.1 THE LIBERAL GOVERNMENT PUBLIC HEALTH MEASURES 1906–11

LEARNING OBJECTIVES

- Understand the key reforms introduced relating to public health
- Analyse attitudes towards government intervention
- Evaluate the impact of these reforms on public health.

SOURCE A

A photograph of a mother, baby and child, 1912. This single room is their bedroom, kitchen and living room.

GOVERNMENT ATTITUDES

Although there were improvements in hygiene and housing during the late 19th century, the general standard of health remained poor for many people. In the years 1891–1903, surveys carried out by Charles Booth and Seebohm Rowntree showed that large numbers of people lived on or below the **poverty line**. This meant that many people lived in poor conditions, where disease spread easily. Poverty also meant poor **nutrition**, which affected people's health; death during childhood was common.

Politicians were also motivated to try to improve the health of the nation when it was found that over one-third of volunteers for the British army during the Boer Wars in Africa (1899–1902) were unfit for service. In some areas, such as the slums of Manchester, the figure was closer to 90 per cent. Since Britain ruled a large **empire**, it needed an effective, well-trained professional army and navy. Therefore, the health and fitness of the nation (especially the men) became important.

When the Liberal Party won a huge majority in the general election of 1906, there was hope that reforms would be introduced. The Liberals seemed

GOVERNMENT ACTION AND WAR — CHANGES IN MEDICINE, c1848–c1948

> ### EXTEND YOUR KNOWLEDGE
>
> In 1888, William Lever founded Port Sunlight, a village near Liverpool, providing good quality accommodation for the workers in his soap factory. During the 1890s, Richard and George Cadbury built Bournville (named after the River Bourn) for their chocolate factory workers. This village had good quality housing and open spaces but George Cadbury believed in avoiding alcohol so there was no pub. Joseph Rowntree established New Earswick, a village for his workers, in 1904.

sympathetic to the concerns of the ordinary people; with a majority in parliament, it seemed the Liberals would easily be able to pass laws to make improvements. Nowadays, we live in a **welfare state**, where we expect the government to use the money from taxes to care for various groups in society and to protect them from the problems associated with poverty. We expect the government to help to provide housing, unemployment benefit, medical treatment and care for the elderly. We also expect the government to make laws so that people are not exploited by their employer or landlord and so that basic standards are met in terms of food and care in schools, hospitals and care homes. The government had a much smaller role at the start of the 20th century, but the Liberal government began to introduce measures which many people see as the beginnings of the modern welfare state.

IMPROVING THE HEALTH OF CHILDREN

SOURCE B

Children in the East End of London queuing for a free meal, c1910.

There was a particular emphasis on helping children to grow up healthy. In 1906, free school meals were introduced for children from poor families. Local authorities received a grant from the government to cover half the cost of these meals, and the number of meals provided increased from 3 million in 1906 to 14 million by 1914. This was a significant move: having at least one proper meal each school day would provide children with the food they needed to support their bodies' growth and to improve their general health.

The Board of Education also produced a booklet which was sent out to schools in 1906. This said children should be taught about hygiene, which would help to reduce the spread of disease.

> **SOURCE C**
>
> From the Board of Education booklet, 1906.
>
> The children should be told that each one of them should have a bath with warm water and soap every week regularly. They should be told that they should wash and brush their teeth and wash their mouths out with clean water both at bedtime and in the morning. They should be told also that their underwear should be changed and washed once a week.

In 1907, the School Medical Service was set up, checking schoolchildren for illness and conditions such as **ringworm** or **lice**. Health Visitors would visit homes to check the health of young children. Unfortunately however, if a health problem was found, many families could not afford to pay for treatment.

The Children and Young Persons Act, 1908, protected children by making it illegal to sell them tobacco or alcohol. This act also made it a crime to send a child out begging or to neglect a child.

OTHER GROUPS IN SOCIETY

Further laws were passed to help other groups in society. In 1908, old age pensions were introduced for people over the age of 70, who earned less than £31.50 per year. They received 25p per week, about one-sixth of a working man's average weekly wage. The pension could be refused if they were alcoholics or if they had been in prison in the previous 10 years.

Only about 600,000 pensions were granted in 1908 but a pension helped those old people to afford housing, food and heating and therefore helped them to stay healthy.

In 1909, Labour Exchanges were set up. These were places where unemployed people could go to look for work. If people had a regular wage, they, and their families, were more likely to be able to eat properly and live in decent accommodation.

THE COST OF PUBLIC HEALTH IMPROVEMENTS

By the early 20th century, people had begun to accept that the central government and local authorities should ensure basic standards of housing and hygiene. But they were not keen to pay for it. There were many complaints when the Liberal government put up taxes in 1909 to pay for its reforms.

But the Liberal government's reforms were very important in improving public health. They showed that the government understood that poor hygiene, living conditions and diet meant that people had little resistance to disease and that when people are living in poverty, they cannot afford treatment for illness.

It is also significant that government accepted the role of protecting the health of the people by taking action to try to prevent them becoming unhealthy. Only parliament had the authority to make these laws and to collect these taxes; local authorities could have organised individual actions, such as providing free school meals or medical inspections for children but local authorities could not have introduced measures to provide pensions and local authorities could not have created a nationwide system of help.

GOVERNMENT ACTION AND WAR — CHANGES IN MEDICINE, c1848–c1948

ACCESS TO TREATMENT

At this time, people had to pay for every visit to the doctor and also for any medicine that was prescribed. This was a particular problem for families close to the poverty line. For this reason, many people avoided seeing a doctor when they became ill and only sought treatment when they became much worse. Unfortunately, by that point, the doctor was often unable to help.

Hospitals in towns and cities usually had free dispensaries where people could go and queue for treatment. However, people often relied on ready-made medicines and pills they could buy from a pharmacist. They also used traditional folk remedies, for example, wrapping your head in brown paper which has been soaked in vinegar to deal with a headache.

Many doctors had created 'sick clubs' where the patient paid a regular amount each week and this money was saved so that it would cover the cost of treatment when necessary. However, ordinary working people could not usually afford to pay into these clubs each week.

THE NATIONAL INSURANCE ACT 1911

In 1911, the government brought in the National Insurance Act. Under the terms of this act, money was paid into the National Insurance Scheme by workers and also by their employers. Any worker who became ill could receive free medical care from a doctor linked to the scheme; they could also claim sickness benefit. A maternity grant was given to help pay for baby essentials. An additional option for workers allowed them to pay into a fund which would provide unemployment benefit if they lost their job.

The introduction of sickness and unemployment benefits was very significant: they could prevent a family falling below the poverty line and allow them to cope if the main wage earner became ill or lost their job.

The act was also important because this was the first time that some groups in society had access to a trained doctor and treatment. It was still not possible to treat many illnesses, especially killer diseases such as tuberculosis and influenza, but treatment could help with the symptoms of many other illnesses. For example, pain relief could be given, some medicines could be prescribed to reduce a patient's fever, ointments could be used to soothe itchy skin and infection could be prevented in an open wound. All these measures meant that a patient was less likely to develop complications during an illness and more likely to survive. Surgery for cases such as appendicitis and tonsillitis also became more common.

Unfortunately, the act only applied to the workers; if members of their families became ill, they could not receive treatment. Furthermore, people who were self-employed or unemployed were not covered.

Figure 4.1 summarises the various measures passed by the Liberal governments from 1906 to 1911, which had an impact on health. These measures mainly applied to the young and the old but the National Insurance Act, 1911, offered support for working men. Women did not benefit very much from these reforms.

SOURCE D

A poster published by the Liberal Party in 1911, showing the benefits of the National Insurance Act.

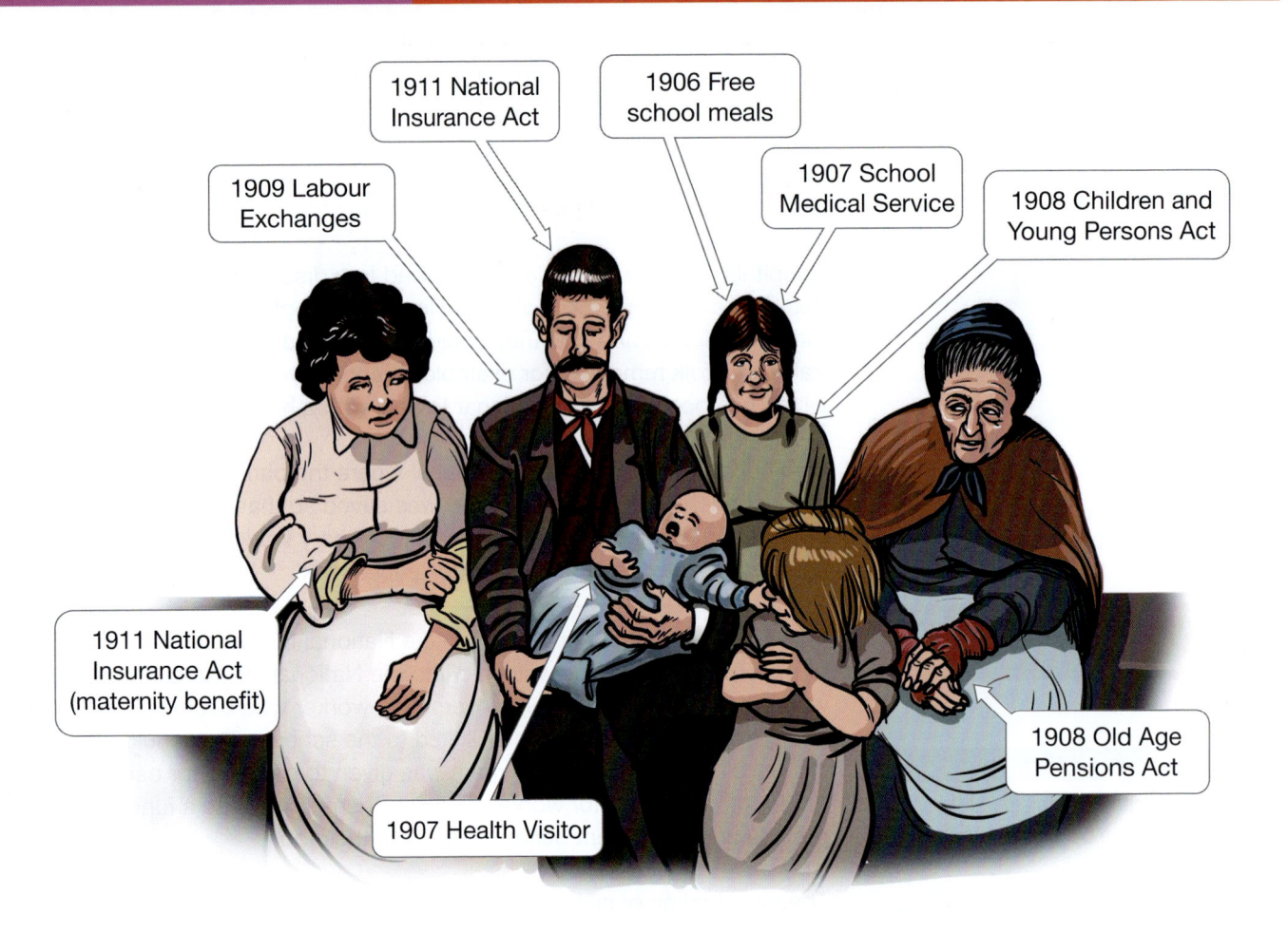

70 GOVERNMENT ACTION AND WAR — CHANGES IN MEDICINE, c1848–c1948

- 1909 Labour Exchanges
- 1911 National Insurance Act
- 1906 Free school meals
- 1907 School Medical Service
- 1908 Children and Young Persons Act
- 1911 National Insurance Act (maternity benefit)
- 1907 Health Visitor
- 1908 Old Age Pensions Act

▲ Figure 4.1 Liberal government reforms

ACTIVITY

1. Explain why the government felt it should pass laws to improve the health of the nation.
2. Make a chart, showing the various acts passed and what they did to improve people's health.
3. Why did some people oppose these new laws?
4. Who do you think benefited most from the Liberal government reforms?

EXAM-STYLE QUESTION

AO1 AO2

Explain **two** ways in which public health provision in Britain from 1905–20 was different from public health provision from 1875–1905. **(6 marks)**

HINT

For each example, provide supporting details to explain clearly what the situation was from 1875–1905 and how it had changed by 1905–20. You will need to read on through the chapter to see other changes up to 1920.

4.2 THE FIRST WORLD WAR

LEARNING OBJECTIVES

- Understand the ways that the war affected developments in medicine
- Analyse changes in the role of women in medicine as a result of the war
- Evaluate the impact of the war on improvements in surgery.

When war broke out in 1914, nobody knew it would become the first 'world war' or that it would last for 4 years. People realised it was significant – because so many European countries were involved, and because these countries had empires stretching around the world – but they still expected the war to be over in a few months.

However, this was a new style of war. By 1914, new weapons (such as more powerful cannon and the machine gun) had been developed and new tactics were needed in battle. It had become very dangerous to be out in the open, so the soldiers dug long trenches to shelter in. By the end of 1914, a system of trenches ran across Belgium and France on what became known as 'the Western Front' of the war. Soon, the war on the Western Front became one where each side tried to overcome the other by using large numbers of soldiers.

Attacks on the enemy's trenches brought huge numbers of casualties and hundreds of thousands of men were wounded or killed. This placed an enormous strain on existing medical services and also led to important developments in treating wounds and illnesses caused by the fighting.

CARE FOR WOUNDED AND SICK SOLDIERS

The First World War led to far more casualties than any previous war. Most injuries were caused by bullets or shrapnel and many wounds became infected because bits of clothing were carried into the wound.

Gangrene was a particular problem. This occurs when the blood supply cannot reach a part of the body; that area of the body becomes gangrenous and begins to rot. The microorganisms causing gangrene produce foul-smelling gas in these wounds. Gangrene was usually fatal.

For the first time, medical teams also had to deal with the effects of poison gas, which was sometimes fired into enemy trenches before an attack. Few soldiers were killed by chlorine or phosgene gas (see Figure 4.2) but they needed to be given oxygen and kept in hospital for up to 2 months. Mustard gas needed different treatment and soldiers needed to bathe with hot soap and water to remove the chemical from their skin. Portable shower units were developed and new clothing was issued. Because mustard gas caused eye injuries, casualties needed to have their eyes washed as quickly as possible. Approximately 186,000 British soldiers were injured by poison gas, with more than 80 per cent caused by mustard gas – approximately 2.6 per cent died.

Chlorine
First used by the Germans in 1915 at the Second Battle of Ypres.

It led to death by suffocation.

The medical services had no experience in dealing with gas attacks, and so had to experiment with treatments.

Gas masks were given to all British troops in July 1915.

Before this, soldiers developed their own system of gas masks. They soaked cotton pads with urine and pressed them to their faces to help stop the gas entering their lungs.

The British retaliated with their own chlorine attack later in 1915 at the Battle of Loos, but the wind changed direction and the gas blew back on the British lines.

Phosgene
First used at the end of 1915 near Ypres.

Its effects were similar to those of chlorine but it was faster acting, killing an exposed person within two days.

Mustard
First used in 1917 by the Germans.

It was an odourless gas that worked within 12 hours, causing both internal and external blisters and could pass through clothing to burn the skin.

▲ Figure 4.2 Three types of poison gas attack on the Western Front

CONDITIONS IN THE TRENCHES

Conditions in the trenches were extremely unhealthy, so soldiers had to deal with disease as well as injuries. Rats in the trenches grew fat eating bits of food but also attacking dead bodies. Many soldiers remember rats running over them as they tried to sleep. Body lice were also a problem; the soldiers could not get rid of the lice until they moved back to base, where they could have a delousing bath and get clean clothes. In some areas of the Western Front, the ground became very muddy when it rained. In these conditions, men developed **trench foot** because they could not keep their feet dry. Clothing was often dirty due to the muddy conditions in the trenches. This made it more likely that wounds would become infected.

EXTEND YOUR KNOWLEDGE

Toilets, called latrines, were usually holes, around 1.5 m deep. Sometimes, however, buckets or even biscuit tins were used. Each day, a layer of chloride of lime was added to cover up the smell. This 'sanitary duty' was often used as a punishment. In bad weather, the latrines sometimes overflowed, with the waste running into the surrounding area.

	▼ MAIN SYMPTOMS	▼ ATTEMPTED SOLUTIONS TO DEAL WITH THE PROBLEM
Trench foot	Painful swelling of the feet, caused by standing in cold mud and water. In the second stage of trench foot, gangrene set in. Gangrene is the decomposition of body tissue due to a loss of blood supply.	■ Prevention was key. ■ Soldiers rubbed whale oil into their feet to protect them. ■ Men tried to keep their feet dry and change their socks regularly. ■ If gangrene developed, amputation was the only solution to stop it spreading along the leg.
Trench fever	Flu-like symptoms with high temperature, headache and aching muscles. This condition was a major problem because it affected an estimated half a million men on the Western Front.	■ By 1918, the cause of trench fever had been identified as contact with lice. Delousing stations were set up. After this, there was a decline in the number of men experiencing the condition.
Shell shock	Symptoms included tiredness, headaches, nightmares, loss of speech, uncontrollable shaking and complete mental breakdown. It has been suggested that about 80,000 British troops experienced shell shock.	■ The condition was not well understood at the time and as a result some soldiers who experienced shell shock were accused of cowardice. Many were punished for this – some were even shot. ■ In some cases, such as Siegfried Sassoon and Wilfred Owen, this involved treatment back in Britain. The Craiglockhart Hospital in Edinburgh treated 2,000 men for shell shock.
Dysentery	A disease causing stomach pains, diarrhoea and sometimes vomiting and fever. The sufferer sometimes died from dehydration. Caused by infected food and water and also by contact with sufferers.	■ The disease spread easily because latrines were unhygienic and soldiers could not always fill their water bottles with clean water and would collect water from shell holes instead, therefore chloride of lime began to be added to purify water but soldiers disliked the taste.

The table above summarises the main medical problems in the trenches.

There were also cases of illness such as influenza, and some soldiers caught sexual infections when they visited prostitutes while on leave.

For all these medical issues, there was little that could be done to treat the illness, apart from providing rest, clean conditions and good food. Remember, at this time there had been little progress in the treatment of illness. The 'magic bullet' Salvarsan 606 was only effective against syphilis, and there was nothing like **penicillin** which could be used to treat infection. Even when soldiers recovered from cases of dysentery or trench fever, they risked reinfection as soon as they returned to the trenches.

GOVERNMENT ACTION AND WAR — CHANGES IN MEDICINE, c1848–c1948

CASUALTY CLEARING STATIONS AND BASE HOSPITALS

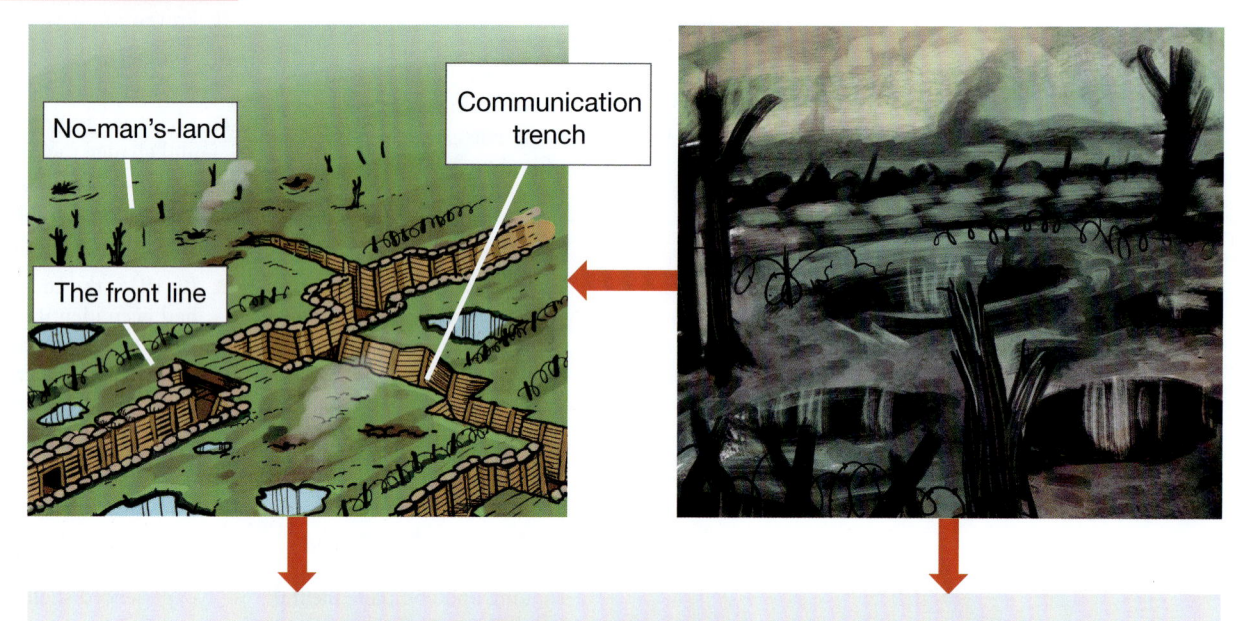

Regimental Aid Posts (RAP) – about 200 m behind the front line

These posts were staffed by a Regimental Medical Officer and stretcher bearers with some knowledge of first aid. These people could give basic first aid but anything more serious was passed further back.

Dressing Stations

An Advanced Dressing Station should have been positioned about 400 m behind the RAP, with a Main Dressing Station about 800 m behind that. Often, there was only a Main Dressing Station.

There would be 10 Medical Officers, some medical assistants (called orderlies) and stretcher bearers. After 1915, there might have been some nurses as well.

Casualty Clearing Station

Anyone with critical injuries or needing more than a few days in hospital would be passed back to the Casualty Clearing Stations, which were further away from the front line.

These clearing stations were often situated close to railway lines so that soldiers with the most severe injuries, who would need extensive care, could be transported back to the better-equipped Base Hospital, or back to Britain.

▲ Figure 4.3 Stages in the treatment of the injured

GOVERNMENT ACTION AND WAR — CHANGES IN MEDICINE, c1848–c1948

ACTIVITY

1. Create a spider diagram showing the injuries and illnesses that occurred during the war.
2. Explain how the conditions in the trenches and the circumstances of war made it difficult to deal with these medical problems.
3. Which do you think was the most important stage in the process of treating wounded soldiers – the first aid posts, Dressing Stations, Casualty Clearing Stations or Base Hospitals?

As Figure 4.3 shows, the British set up a system of treatment centres to help casualties at the front. Immediate aid was given at Regimental First Aid Posts (RAP), more advanced help at **Dressing Stations** and soldiers with critical injuries were treated at Casualty Clearing Stations. The most severe cases would be transported to Base Hospitals behind the lines. During the war, it became clear that the effects of poison gas and the chance of infection in a wound were reduced if surgery was carried out as soon as possible. As a result, medical staff began to carry out more operations at the Casualty Clearing Stations, while Base Hospitals became responsible for longer term treatment. Base Hospitals also began to group patients according to their injuries and to allocate doctors to each ward, so doctors began to specialise in specific types of injury.

In both Casualty Clearing Stations and Base Hospitals, the nature of the injuries forced doctors to experiment with new techniques. At Casualty Clearing Stations, surgeons had to deal with horrific head and chest wounds caused by the use of explosives. Instead of a single bullet wound, explosives would spray shrapnel in all directions, causing multiple wounds; although these injuries were often not fatal immediately, many soldiers died from infection later if there was no X-ray machine to locate each piece of shrapnel.

THE WORK OF THE RAMC AND OF THE NURSES

KEY TERM

front the area in a war where fighting is taking place

The Royal Army Medical Corps (RAMC) was the section of the army that dealt with injured soldiers. It organised treatment for the wounded at first aid posts, close to the **front**. It also ran Dressing Stations and hospitals.

SOURCE E

An Advanced Dressing Station in France, 1918. The artist, Henry Tonks, was a British surgeon. This painting shows the types of injury suffered by the soldiers and the work of the Royal Army Medical Corps.

GOVERNMENT ACTION AND WAR — CHANGES IN MEDICINE, c1848–c1948

The main group of trained nurses working with the army was the Queen Alexandra's Imperial Military Nursing Service (QAIMNS). This had been founded in 1902 and there were fewer than 300 nurses in 1914. By 1918, however, there were over 10,000 trained nurses. Another set of nurses who worked with the RAMC belonged to the First Aid Nursing Yeomanry (FANY), which had been founded in 1907. The idea was that women who joined FANY would be first aid specialists but would also have skills that would allow them to get to casualties on the battlefield itself. Therefore, the original members of FANY were trained in signalling and camping out.

WOMEN AS VOLUNTEERS

The high number of casualties during the First World War meant that the RAMC needed even more additional help. We have already seen that Marie Curie drove an ambulance for the French army, collecting wounded soldiers from the front. British women also volunteered to help. Many women joined the Women's Army Auxiliary Corps, which was set up in 1917. These women acted as ambulance drivers, among other duties.

Branches of the Red Cross organisation sent out Voluntary Aid Detachments (VADs) who also drove ambulances and acted as nurses in the RAMC hospitals. These nurses were usually middle-class single women, with little relevant experience. In hospitals, they mainly helped with basic tasks: cleaning floors, changing bed linen and cleaning out **bedpans**.

Although individual training schools kept lists of their students, there was no official register for nurses until 1919. Therefore, we do not know how many women were trained nurses and how many volunteered to work as nurses without proper training. Trained nurses often disliked working with volunteers because they felt that their qualifications would not be respected. Nevertheless, the contribution of these different groups of women was vital.

SOURCE F

From an account written by a VAD, published in 1933.

Sometimes in the middle of the night we have to turn people out of bed and make them sleep on the floor to make room for the more seriously ill ones who have come. The strain is very, very great. The enemy is within shelling distance – aeroplanes carrying machine guns – ambulance trains jolting into the siding, all day, all night – gassed men on stretchers clawing the air – dying men reeking with mud and foul green stained bandages, shrieking and writhing in a grotesque travesty of manhood – dead men with fixed empty eyes and shiny yellow faces

SOURCE G

A photograph showing the inside of an ambulance train. It was built in 1916 to bring wounded soldiers away from the Western Front.

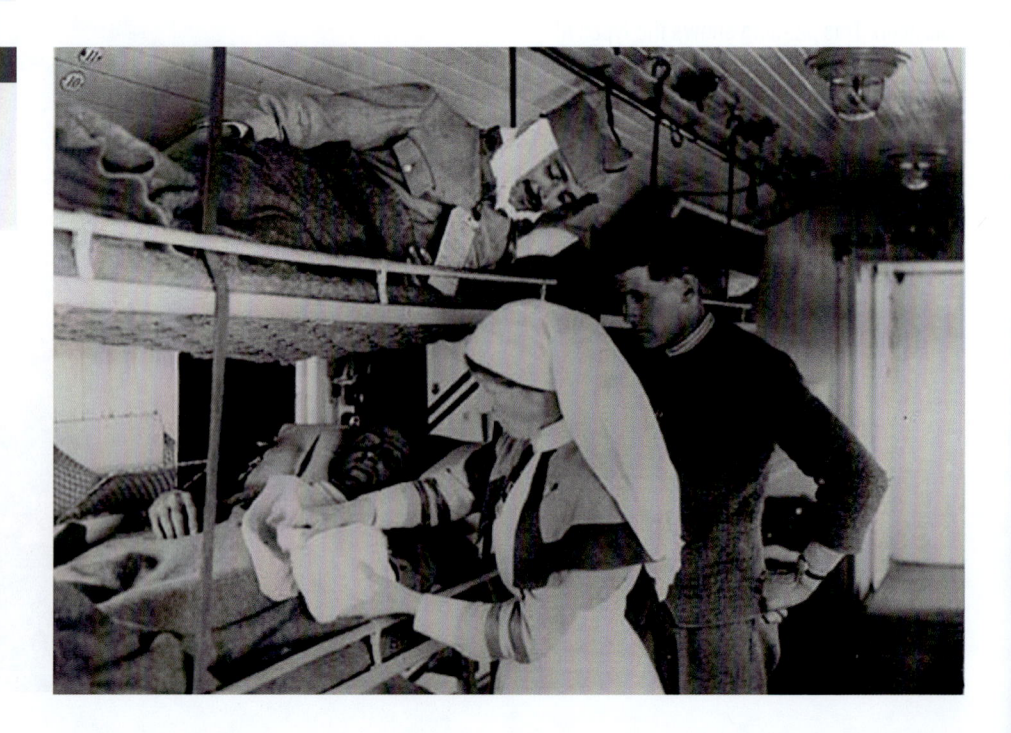

WOMEN DOCTORS

Despite the achievements of women such as Elizabeth Garrett, and the 1876 Act which allowed women to gain a medical degree, female doctors who wanted to volunteer to help on the Western Front were not usually welcomed.

Dr Elsie Inglis offered to take women's medical units to the Front and to create a 100-bed hospital. However, she was told that '**hysterical** women' were the last people they wanted there. Dr Louisa Garrett (daughter of Elizabeth) and Dr Flora Murray founded the Women's Hospital Corps, but had to open military hospitals in Paris and near Boulogne before they could get permission to open one in London. Mabel Stobart founded a hospital staffed only by women – but it was in Belgium.

At the start of the war, the War Office believed it had enough male doctors to deal with the casualties of war and refused to employ women doctors in war zones. However, various agencies sent medical supplies and teams to help and many of these were willing to include women.

ACTIVITY

1. What can you learn from Sources E and F about the work of the RAMC and nurses on the Western Front?
2. What can you learn from Sources G and H about the way nurses and doctors had to adapt to the conditions of war?

SOURCE H

A letter from Louisa Garrett Anderson to her mother, written in 1914. She was describing how they set up a hospital in France, which was based in a hotel.

The hotel was a gorgeous shell of marble and gilt without heating or crockery or anything practical. The cases that come to us are very septic and the wounds are terrible. We have fitted up quite a satisfactory small operating theatre in the 'Ladies Lavatory' which has tiled floor and walls, good water supply and heating. I bought a simple operating table in Paris. It is very exhilarating to be on top of the wave, helped and approved by everyone, except perhaps the English War Office.

VOLUNTARY HOSPITALS

EXTEND YOUR KNOWLEDGE

Millicent Leveson-Gower, Duchess of Sutherland, had been called 'Meddlesome Millie' when she campaigned for better working conditions and to have the lead paint removed from local pottery manufacture. In 1914, she organised an ambulance unit that saw active service in Belgium. For a short while, she was trapped behind enemy lines but managed to escape back to England. She then travelled to France, where she helped to set up field hospitals. After the war, she was awarded the French Croix de Guerre, the Belgian Royal Red Cross medal, and the British Red Cross medal.

Many of the early volunteers were from rich and powerful families, such as the Duchess of Sutherland. These women were used to running large households and family estates. When the British War Office did not want their help, they organised transport to France and Belgium, taking nurses and equipment to set up hospitals and Casualty Clearing Stations.

Mairi Chisholm and Elsie Knocker travelled to Belgium to join a small ambulance corps set up by Dr Hector Munro. Many soldiers were dying because the Base Hospital was so far from the front lines that they could not be treated soon enough. So the two women decided to set up a first aid post in Pervyse, approximately 100 metres away from the Belgian frontline; grateful soldiers nicknamed them 'Angels of Pervyse'.

The largest voluntary hospital in France, and one of the hospitals closest to the front line, was run by Dr Frances Ivens. It had over 600 beds and an excellent X-ray unit, which was important for locating bullets and shrapnel before surgery. Between January 1915 and February 1919 the surgeons performed 7,204 operations.

SOURCE I

An account by Dr Elizabeth Courtauld, May 1918, describing conditions at Villers-Cotterêts.

Terrible cases came in. Between 10.30 and 3.30 or 4 a.m. we had to amputate six thighs and one leg, mostly by the light of bits of candle, held by the orderlies, and as for me giving the anaesthetic, I did it more or less in the dark at my end of the patient.

GREATER ACCEPTANCE OF WOMEN?

At the start of the war less than 1 per cent of doctors were female and most general hospitals did not accept women doctors, so their medical experience was as General Practitioners or in hospitals specifically for women and children. Very few had any experience of surgery beyond their initial medical training course.

Although the work of nurses and VADs became welcome, the War Office told female doctors to stay at home and cover the gaps created by male doctors leaving to work at the Front. However, the nature of fighting on the Western Front created heavy casualties and in 1916 the army asked for medical women to work with the RAMC in Malta, an island in the Mediterranean Sea which was used as a central medical area for casualties; by the end of the year, there were 80 female doctors working in Malta. Even then, women doctors did not receive the same treatment as men. Male doctors who worked with the RAMC automatically became temporary army officers – but women did not.

WOMEN IN MEDICINE ON THE HOME FRONT

Over half of the doctors in Britain entered the army. This created a demand for medical staff back in Britain. Hospitals needed to replace the male staff who had gone to support the army. In addition, new military hospitals were set up in Britain to provide care for severely wounded soldiers.

In 1915, Louisa Garrett Anderson and Flora Murray were placed in charge of a new military hospital in London, staffed entirely by women. The hospital staff included 15 doctors, surgeons, ophthalmic surgeons, dental surgeons, an anaesthetist, bacteriological experts and seven assistant doctors and surgeons, together with a full staff of women assistants.

SOURCE J
A plaque in memory of the work of Flora Murray and Louisa Garrett Anderson at Endell Street Military Hospital in London.

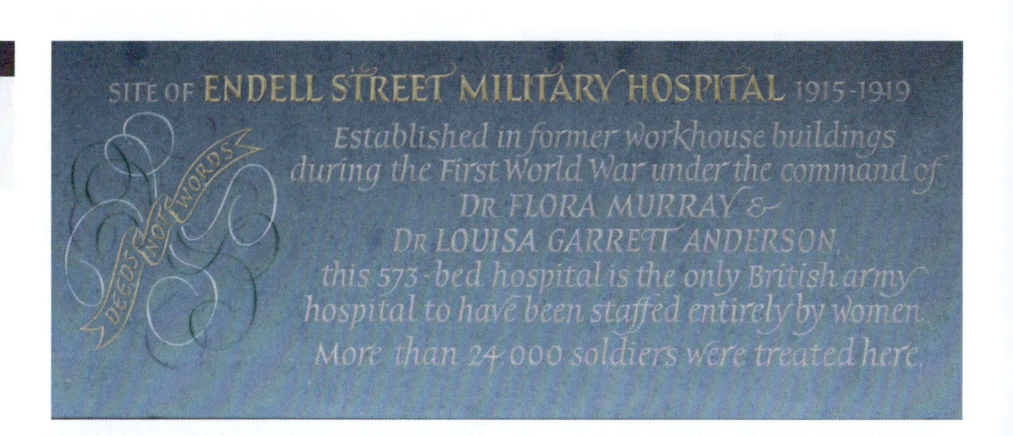

SITE OF ENDELL STREET MILITARY HOSPITAL 1915-1919
Established in former workhouse buildings during the First World War under the command of DR FLORA MURRAY & DR LOUISA GARRETT ANDERSON, this 573-bed hospital is the only British army hospital to have been staffed entirely by women. More than 24,000 soldiers were treated here.
DEEDS NOT WORDS

The shortage of doctors during the war meant that attitudes changed towards women doctors but this change was only temporary. Although approximately one-fifth of women doctors had carried out hospital work, often abroad, they found it difficult to be given positions within hospitals after the war and they were expected to return to their role as GPs.

| GOVERNMENT ACTION AND WAR | CHANGES IN MEDICINE, c1848–c1948 | 79 |

ACTIVITY

1 Create a chart showing the range of different roles played by women in medicine during the war.
2 Why do you think there was so much resistance to women's involvement in medicine, even after the war?

Meanwhile, 12 London hospital schools began to accept women students during the war and the London School of Medicine for Women became the largest medical school in the country. It is believed that there were 610 qualified women doctors in 1911 and 1,500 by 1921. However, after the war, women medical students were once again often rejected and the Royal Free Hospital was the only London teaching hospital accepting women students.

The government encouraged women to volunteer their help in Britain and thousands of untrained women worked as midwives or nurses, but here also their lack of training and qualifications meant that they were often regarded almost as servants.

EXAM-STYLE QUESTION

A01 **A02**

SKILLS: PROBLEM SOLVING, REASONING, DECISION MAKING

How far was the First World War responsible for changes in the role of women in medicine in the years 1875–1920?

You may use the following information to help you with your answer:
- Medical Act 1876
- VADs during the First World War.

You **must** also use information of your own. **(16 marks)**

HINT
This question offers one reason why women's position in medicine changed during this period. You need to find evidence to support that idea and evidence to challenge it before you can make a judgement.

4.3 IMPROVEMENTS IN SURGERY

LEARNING OBJECTIVES

- Understand the improvements that occurred in surgery as a result of the war
- Analyse the role of science and technology in these changes
- Evaluate the impact of the war on medicine and surgery.

X-RAYS

We have already seen that X-rays were important in surgery, especially when dealing with wounds during the war. Base Hospitals and some Casualty Clearing Stations had X-ray machines. In addition, Marie Curie had developed mobile X-ray machines and six similar units were in use in the British section of the Western Front.

By taking two X-rays from different angles, the surgeon was able to locate any metal in a wound very precisely. However, there were some problems that prevented X-rays being used to their full potential.
- X-rays could not be used to identify fragments of clothing within a wound.
- The wounded person had to remain still for some time while the X-ray was taken. This was often a problem when soldiers were in pain.
- The glass tubes used in X-ray machines often overheated after about an hour, so the machines could not be in continuous use.
- The high dose of radiation used in an X-ray was harmful and could cause burns (although the danger was not fully understood at this time).

80 GOVERNMENT ACTION AND WAR — CHANGES IN MEDICINE, c1848–c1948

SOURCE K
A photograph taken in 1917 of a mobile X-ray unit.

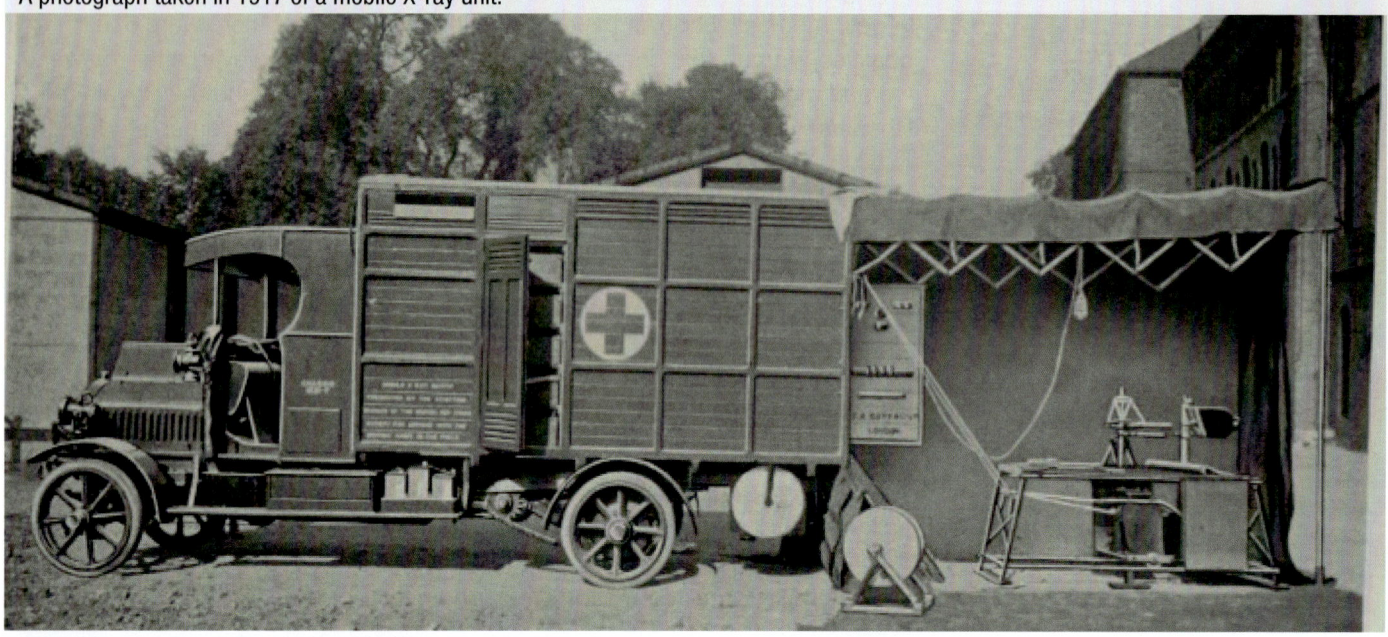

BLOOD TRANSFUSIONS

Blood loss was a major problem during the war; many soldiers died from blood loss even though their injuries would not have been fatal otherwise. Improved scientific knowledge had made blood transfusions possible before the war. However, the donor had to be present so transfusions were not very practical in wartime. The huge number of casualties in the war increased the need for blood transfusions. As a result, various scientists experimented with ways to prevent blood clotting and increase the time that it could be stored.

The table below summarises the key stages in the development of blood transfusions and storage.

▶ 1901	Karl Landsteiner discovered that blood transfusions would only work if the donor and the patient had blood from the same blood group. Later it was discovered that blood from group O can be safely given to anyone.	This meant that person-to-person transfusions became possible.
▶ 1915	The American doctor Richard Lewisohn discovered that adding sodium citrate would stop blood clotting.	This meant that blood could be collected and stored, ready for use in an emergency. However, the blood cells deteriorated if they were not used within a few days.
▶ 1915	Richard Weil found that blood could be stored for slightly longer if it was refrigerated.	This made it possible to store larger volumes of blood. Transfusions could now be used on a greater scale, as long as the blood was stored correctly.
▶ 1915	The Canadian doctor, Lawrence Bruce Robertson, pioneered the use of indirect transfusion. In this process, blood was transfused into the patient (through a syringe and a tube) **before** surgery.	This improved the patient's chances of surviving the surgery. However, it also increased the demand for blood.
▶ 1916	Francis Rous and James Turner found that adding glucose citrate increased the time blood could be stored, up to 4 weeks.	This meant that stores of blood could be built up before a major battle. This would increase the chances of survival for injured soldiers.
▶ 1917	Battle of Cambrai. Blood depots of type O blood were created before the battle.	This increased the survival rate among soldiers who were not transferred back to a Casualty Clearing Station.

NEW TECHNIQUES IN SURGERY

Surgeons knew that any delay in operation increased the chances of infection, especially if there was **gas gangrene** in the wound. However, it was impossible to recreate the aseptic conditions of a London hospital when working in a Dressing Station or Casualty Clearing Station. For example, there were so many casualties that injured men were often left on the floor because there were not enough beds.

It was recognised that infected tissue needed to be removed as soon as possible and that the wound needed to be thoroughly cleansed. Various different techniques were developed. The procedure called 'excision' or 'debridement' involved cutting away infected tissue so that all danger of gangrene was removed. It was also noted that feeding a sterilised salt solution through the wound could be effective, but both of these methods were time-consuming procedures. If this was not done thoroughly enough or soon enough, amputation was the only way to prevent the spread of infection.

Wound excision or debridement
This was the cutting away of dead, damaged and infected tissue from around the site of the wound. It needed to be done as soon as possible because infection could spread quickly. After excision, the wound needed to be closed by stitching. If any infected tissue had not been removed before the wound was stitched, the infection would spread again.

The Carrel-Dakin method
Antiseptics, such as carbolic lotion, were inefficient when treating gas gangrene. By 1917, it was agreed that the Carrel-Dakin method, which involved using a sterilised salt solution in the wound through a tube, was the most effective alternative. The solution only lasted for 6 hours and so had to be made as it was needed. This could be difficult, especially when large numbers of wounded men needed treatment at the same time.

Amputation
If neither wound excision nor the use of antiseptics succeeded in halting the spread of infection, the only way to deal with it was through the amputation of wounded limbs. By 1918, 240,000 men had lost limbs – many of them because it was the only way to prevent the spread of infection and death.

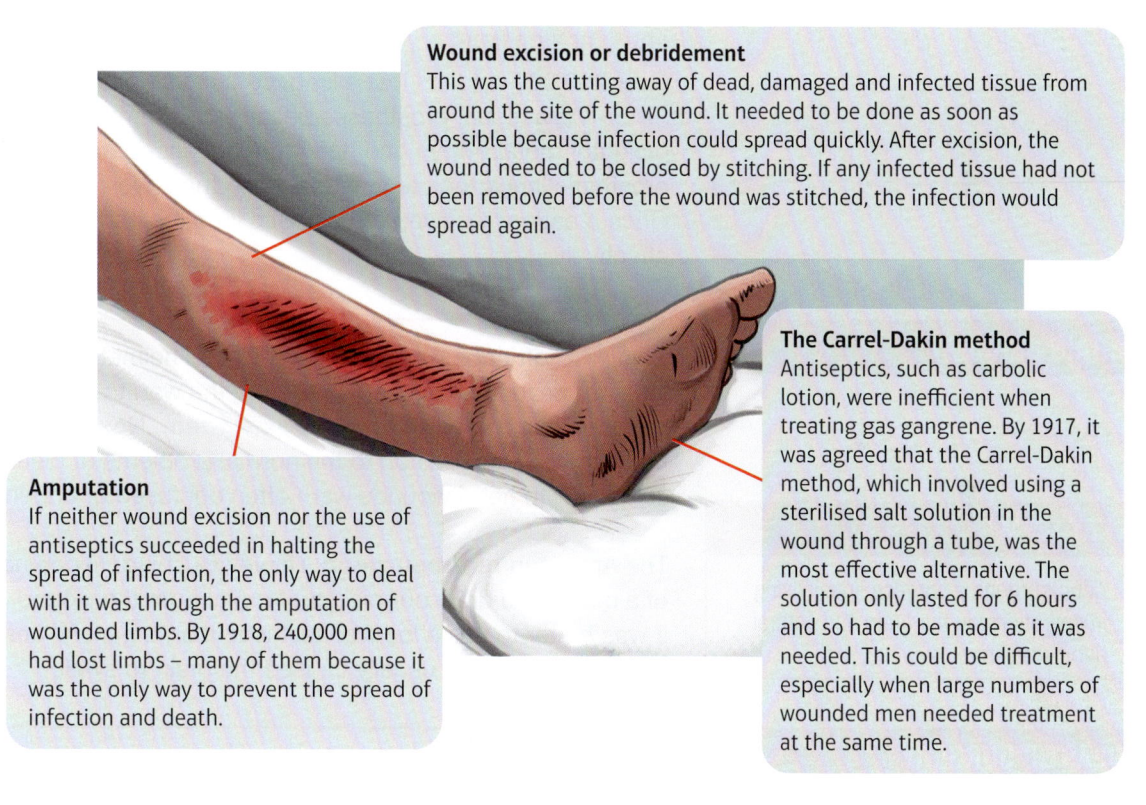

▲ Figure 4.4 The main techniques used to prevent the spread of infection

THE THOMAS SPLINT

Another problem was that broken bones could break through the skin and create an open wound. Broken limbs should be kept as still and straight as possible until a surgeon could operate. However, injured men had to be carried back from the front line to a Casualty Clearing Station, and injuries were often made worse as the patient was moved. In many cases, by the time a soldier with a leg wound reached the Casualty Clearing Station, the best option was to have the leg amputated. Otherwise, the soldier would probably die from infection, bleeding or gas gangrene.

Robert Jones worked in a London hospital. He used an idea developed by his uncle, Hugh Thomas, to keep the leg still. This helped to prevent further problems. The Thomas splint was introduced on the Western Front at the end of 1915. After its introduction, the survival rate for this type of wound improved from 20 per cent to 82 per cent.

Figure 4.5 The Thomas splint

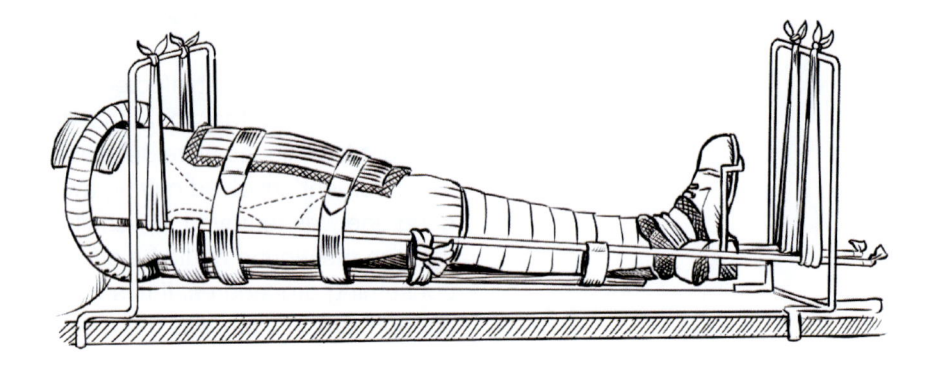

PROSTHETIC LIMBS

Over 240,000 soldiers lost a limb, so there was a huge need for **prosthetic limbs**. As a result, prostheses became much more advanced: they were made of lighter metal **alloys** and had more advanced **mechanisms**. However, these prosthetic limbs took time to make, so there were long waiting lists for them. Once a patient received a prosthetic limb, he had to be taught how to use it effectively.

BRAIN SURGERY

Soldiers' soft caps were replaced by steel helmets in 1915, but many soldiers suffered head injuries even so. Before the war, there had been little surgery on the brain and the **central nervous system**. Now, surgeons had to deal with these injuries. In addition to the normal problems of bleeding and infection, soldiers with head wounds were often confused or unconscious.

KEY TERM

neurosurgeon a surgeon specialising in operations on the brain and central nervous system

The American **neurosurgeon**, Harvey Cushing, experimented with the use of a magnet to draw out pieces of metal from the wound. He also found that it was better to use a local anaesthetic than a general anaesthetic, since a general anaesthetic usually caused the brain to swell.

PLASTIC SURGERY

Head injuries also caused terrible non-fatal wounds. Facial bones could be smashed or eyes could be lost, and men could be left with gaping holes in their faces. The New Zealand doctor, Harold Gillies, experimented with new techniques, such as using pieces of bone or cartilage to create new features (for example, a new nose made from a piece of bone). He tried to repair facial injuries, so that the patient's appearance would be as close to normal as possible. (The alternative was for the patient to wear a painted mask to hide their injuries.)

Surgeons before the war had developed the use of skin grafts – taking tissue from one part of the body and using it to repair an injury to another part of the body. However, these skin grafts were often rejected by the body. Gillies felt that skin grafts would be more successful if the blood flow to the grafted tissue was maintained. He developed a technique called the pedicle tube; using this technique, a flap of skin was 'grown' until it could be attached to a new part of the body.

This required several operations over a long period of time, so patients had to be treated in England. Gillies set up a **plastic surgery** unit at the Queen's Hospital in Sidcup, Kent in 1917. Nearly 12,000 operations were carried out before the end of the war in 1918.

▶ Figure 4.6 The development of plastic surgery

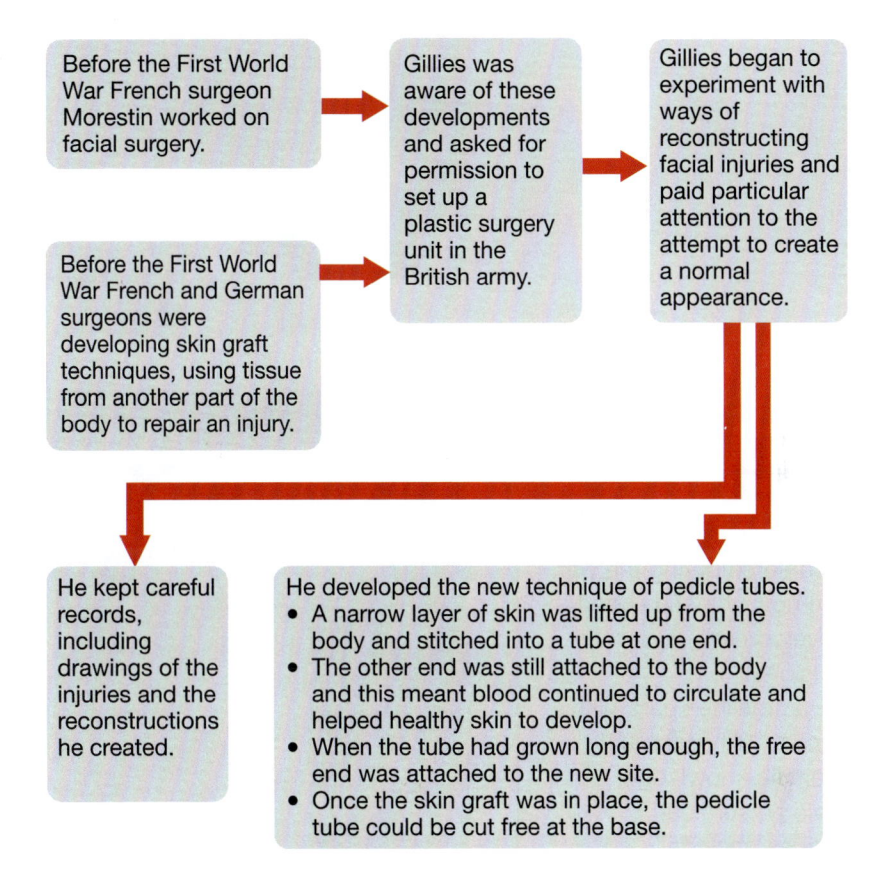

- Before the First World War French surgeon Morestin worked on facial surgery.
- Before the First World War French and German surgeons were developing skin graft techniques, using tissue from another part of the body to repair an injury.

→ Gillies was aware of these developments and asked for permission to set up a plastic surgery unit in the British army.

→ Gillies began to experiment with ways of reconstructing facial injuries and paid particular attention to the attempt to create a normal appearance.

→ He kept careful records, including drawings of the injuries and the reconstructions he created.

→ He developed the new technique of pedicle tubes.
- A narrow layer of skin was lifted up from the body and stitched into a tube at one end.
- The other end was still attached to the body and this meant blood continued to circulate and helped healthy skin to develop.
- When the tube had grown long enough, the free end was attached to the new site.
- Once the skin graft was in place, the pedicle tube could be cut free at the base.

84 GOVERNMENT ACTION AND WAR — CHANGES IN MEDICINE, c1848–c1948

SOURCE L

Photographs showing the facial reconstruction of a soldier whose cheek was extensively wounded during the Battle of the Somme, 1916.

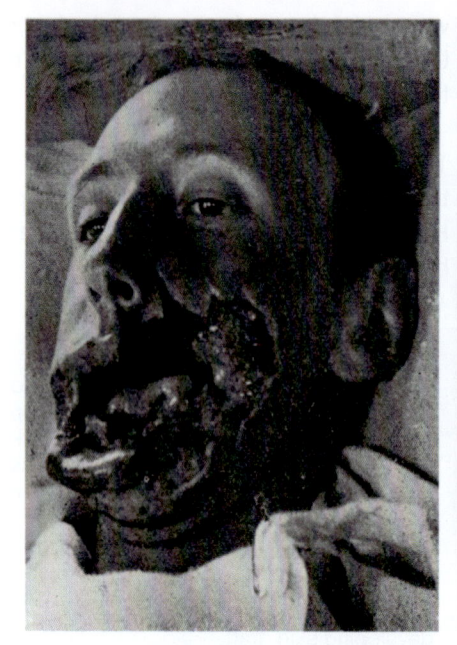

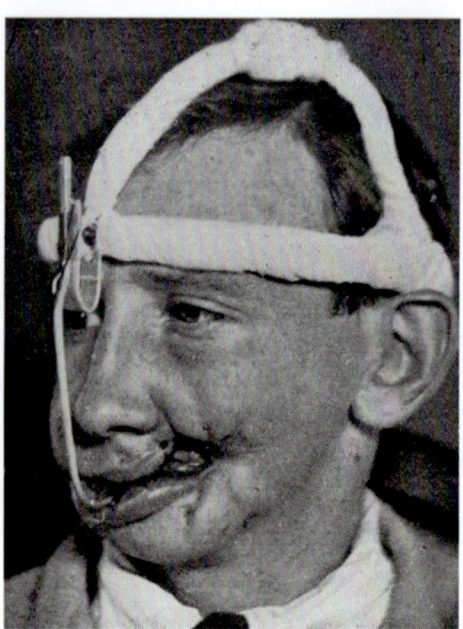

ACTIVITY

1. Explain why surgeons faced new problems during the war.
2. Explain how war stimulated the development of blood transfusions.
3. Create a timeline chart, with columns for developments in: scientific knowledge; technology; surgical techniques. Include developments in blood transfusions, X-rays, and surgery.

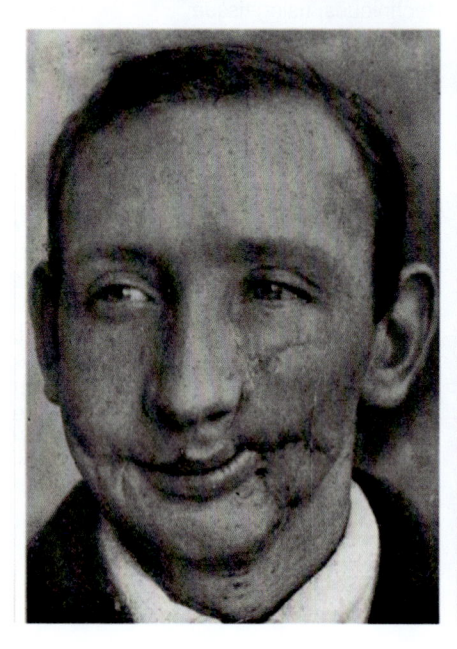

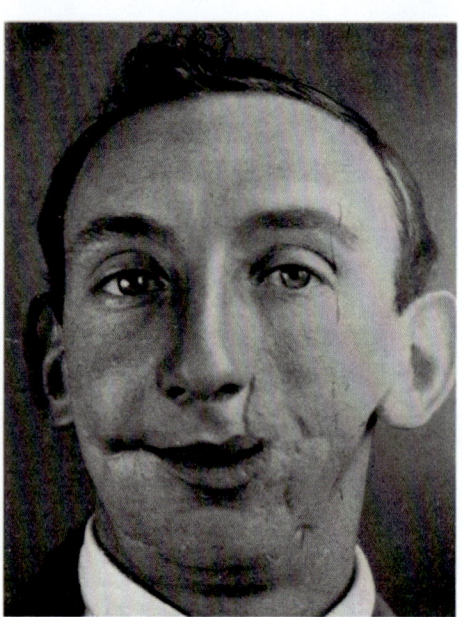

EXAM-STYLE QUESTION

Explain **two** causes of improvements in surgery from 1905–20. **(8 marks)**

A01 A02

SKILLS ADAPTIVE LEARNING

HINT

Make sure you explain clearly the link between each of the reasons you give and a specific improvement in surgery.

RECAP

RECALL QUIZ

1. Name one act passed by the Liberal government to help children become healthier.
2. Why was there opposition to Lloyd George's introduction of pensions?
3. Who was helped by the National Insurance Act 1911?
4. Who did not benefit from the National Insurance Act 1911?
5. What was the RAMC?
6. Name three medical conditions that affected soldiers during the war.
7. What was the role of VADs and FANYs?
8. Why did the war lead to an increased number of female doctors?
9. State two ways in which technology improved the standard of surgery during the war.
10. Give two examples of areas of surgery where progress was stimulated by the war.

CHECKPOINT

STRENGTHEN
S1 Explain why the government wanted to improve the health of the nation.
S2 Explain how the Liberal government reforms aimed to create a healthier nation.
S3 Explain the types of injury that soldiers suffered during the war.

CHALLENGE
C1 How much impact did the Liberal government reforms have on public health?
C2 How much did the position of women in medicine change during 1905–20?
C3 In what area of surgery did the First World War lead to most progress?

SUMMARY

- There was a change of attitude to the government's role in public health. Greater **intervention** was now accepted.
- The Liberal governments, from 1905–11, passed a series of acts intended to help people become healthier.
- There were still some groups who were not helped by these reforms.
- There was little development in medical treatment even though the first magic bullet was discovered.
- The First World War produced a range of new injuries. Doctors and surgeons were forced to develop new techniques as they tried to deal with these injuries.
- A series of treatment stages was developed to try to ensure injuries were treated as quickly as possible.
- Women played an important role in medicine, both on the Western Front and at home. However, there was little overall change in their position in medicine.
- X-rays were important in locating bullets and shrapnel.
- Developments in blood transfusions led to an increased survival rate.
- There were developments in both brain surgery and plastic surgery.

EXAM GUIDANCE: PART (A) QUESTIONS

A01 **A02**

Question to be answered: Explain two ways in which the role of women in medicine was similar in 1876 and the First World War (1914–18). (6 marks)

1 **Analysis Question 1: What is the question type testing?**
In this question you have to demonstrate that you have knowledge and understanding of the key features and characteristics of the period studied. In this particular case it is knowledge and understanding of the role of women in 1876 and the role of women in the war.

You also have to explain, analyse and make judgements about historical events and periods to explain ways in which there were similarities between those times.

2 **Analysis Question 2: What do I have to do to answer the question well?**
Obviously you have to write about the role of women in medicine but it isn't just a case of writing everything you know. You have to identify two similarities and provide detail showing the ways in which women's role in medicine in one period was similar to women's role in medicine in the other period. If you just write about women's role in medicine, you are unlikely to do that clearly. So you should start by identifying ways in which they are similar and then providing detail to prove it. If you were planning this answer, you would have a subheading of 'first similarity', followed by details from 1876 and details from the period 1914–18, then a subheading of 'second similarity', followed by details from each period.

So in this case, you could consider women's role as nurses and women's role as doctors. You will get 1 mark for each similarity you show, 1 mark for explaining that similarity and another mark for detail. Rather than say very similar things about the work women did as nurses and as doctors, it would be a good idea to show the increasing professionalisation of nurses and the increasing number of women becoming doctors and then to consider the effects of working as nurses and doctors during the First World War (1914–1918).

3 **Analysis Question 3: Are there any techniques I can use to make it very clear that I am doing what is needed to be successful?**
This is a 6-mark question and you need to make sure you leave enough time to answer the other two questions fully (they are worth 24 marks in total). This is not an essay and you don't need to give a general introduction or conclusion. However, it is helpful to structure your answer as two separate paragraphs, making it clear to the examiner that you are explaining two similarities. It's a good idea to write two paragraphs and to begin each paragraph with phrases like 'One similarity was…', 'Another similarity was…'. You will get a maximum of 3 marks for each similarity you explain, so make sure you do two similarities.

Note: The question does not ask 'How similar' so you do not have to point out similarities and differences. Just stick to similarities.

Answer A
The role of women as nurses in the years 1876 and 1914–18 was very similar. In both periods they cared for the sick in hospitals. The training of nurses had been begun by Florence Nightingale, who had done a lot of work at the army medical hospital in Scutari during the Crimean War. Another similarity was that women increasingly began to qualify as doctors and to work in hospitals and as General Practitioners. This can be seen in the year 1876 and increased during the years 1914–18.

What are the strengths and weaknesses of Answer A?
This answer states two similarities but there is very little supporting detail to prove that it is a valid comment.

This is typical of a Level 1 answer: it is about the general topic (women in medicine) and has no specific examples of what was similar; the supporting detail, although accurate, is not relevant to this question.

Answer B
Women's role as nurses in hospitals was similar during both periods. Training was based on the work of Florence Nightingale and the role of nurses had become much more important in the care of the sick in hospitals by 1876, especially as more operations began to be carried out. This situation continued, especially during the First World War, when many nurses worked with the RAMC at Advanced Dressing Stations and Casualty Clearing Stations and they also worked at Base Hospitals, carrying out the treatment prescribed by a doctor for the injured and sick soldiers.

Another similarity was the role of women as doctors. After the Act of 1876 women began to qualify as doctors in Britain and to work as General Practitioners and in hospitals, although there were relatively few of them. However, during the First World War, female doctors worked both on the Western Front, dealing with injured soldiers, and in Britain, filling the gaps in hospitals where the male doctors had gone to serve with the army.

So these two examples show that the role of women as nurses and doctors was very similar in 1875 and 1914–18.

What are the strengths and weaknesses of Answer B?
This is an excellent answer. Each paragraph begins by stating a similarity and then provides supporting detail from each period to explain the similarity in more detail. It would be likely to receive full marks.

Challenge a friend
Use the Student Book to set a part (a) question for a friend. Then look at the answer. Does it do the following things?

- ☐ Identify two similarities
- ☐ Provide supporting detail about each period to show what was similar.

If it does, you can tell your friend that the answer is very good!

5. ADVANCES IN MEDICINE, SURGERY AND PUBLIC HEALTH, 1920–48

LEARNING OBJECTIVES

- Understand the importance of the development of penicillin
- Understand the impact on medicine and surgery of the Second World War
- Understand the importance of the creation of the National Health Service.

The period of 1920–48 was very important in medicine for several reasons.

Since the discovery of of Salvarsan 606 scientists had been looking for a second 'magic bullet'. In 1932 they found it. Even more importantly, in this period the antibiotic penicillin was developed. Penicillin would transform medicine.

In surgery, the ability to store blood for transfusions had been extremely important in dealing with injuries during the First World War; this now had a big impact on other operations and illnesses.

New techniques had been developed during the First World War for dealing with wounds and broken limbs and after the war more advances were made in prosthetics, neurosurgery and plastic surgery. Many more advances were made during the Second World War, particularly in these new areas of surgery.

The work of the government in improving the health of the nation had expanded during the early 20th century, with the government offering more support to ensure people could stay healthy. Government action now widened even further. During the 1920s and 1930s, the government began to organise hospitals into a national system and then set up the National Health Service to make access to medical care freely available at all stages of life.

5.1 THE DEVELOPMENT OF PENICILLIN

LEARNING OBJECTIVES

- Understand the work of Fleming, Florey and Chain in the discovery and development of penicillin
- Analyse the factors affecting the development of penicillin
- Evaluate the roles played by Fleming, Florey and Chain.

FLEMING'S DISCOVERY

During the First World War, a doctor called Alexander Fleming had worked in a military hospital in Boulogne, in France. He had seen the problems caused by infections such as **septicaemia** and gangrene in deep wounds; he also knew that ordinary antiseptics were ineffective against these infections. He realised that there was a need for a new treatment – like the magic bullet, Salvarsan 606 – to fight the microorganisms causing infections.

After the war, Fleming returned to his work as a medical researcher at St Mary's Hospital in London. In 1922, he discovered that the **enzyme** lysosome, which can be found in tears and other body fluids, kills many microorganisms; unfortunately, it only kills harmless microorganisms, not those which cause disease or infection. Fleming wrote articles about his work. However, the laboratory in which he worked was focused on developing vaccines, so he did not pursue his research on lysosome any further.

In 1928, Fleming became Professor of Bacteriology at St Mary's Hospital Medical School. He was well known for his research – and also for his untidy methods! He had been studying **staphylococcus** cultures; when he went on holiday, he left the cultures piled in a corner of his laboratory. When he returned, he found that one of the cultures had been contaminated with a **mould**. He noticed that the staphylococcus culture had been destroyed in the area around the mould.

SOURCE A

A photograph of the original culture plate on which Fleming observed the growth of penicillin. The note on the photograph draws attention to the large penicillin colony at the top and the reduced amount of the original staphylococcus culture.

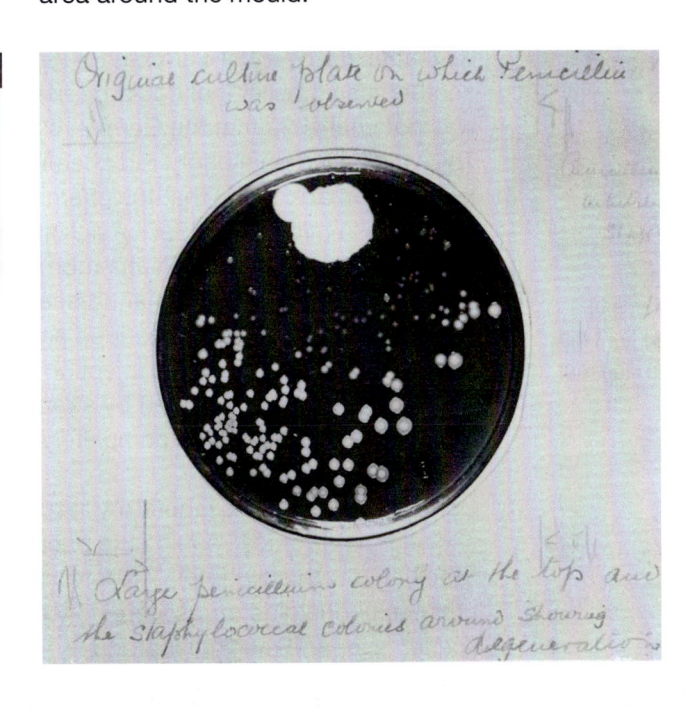

ADVANCES, 1920–48 — CHANGES IN MEDICINE, c1848–c1948

WAS THE DISCOVERY OF PENICILLIN A BREAKTHROUGH?

Fleming grew the mould in a pure culture and found that it could be used to kill various microorganisms which caused disease. He identified the mould as part of the penicillium **genus** and named it penicillin. This was different from magic bullets because it was not based on chemicals. Instead, it was an **antibiotic**, using bacteria to attack other bacteria.

In fact, penicillin was not really a new discovery. During the Middle Ages, people knew that mouldy bread was sometimes effective against infection if it was spread onto a wound, although no one could explain why. In 1871, Joseph Lister had used penicillium to treat a nurse at King's College Hospital, after her wound did not respond to any antiseptic. Louis Pasteur and Ernest Duchesne had also noticed that various types of penicillium were effective against infection. So Fleming's 'discovery' did not seem to be a particularly significant breakthrough.

SOURCE B

Paintings done by Fleming, using microorganisms.

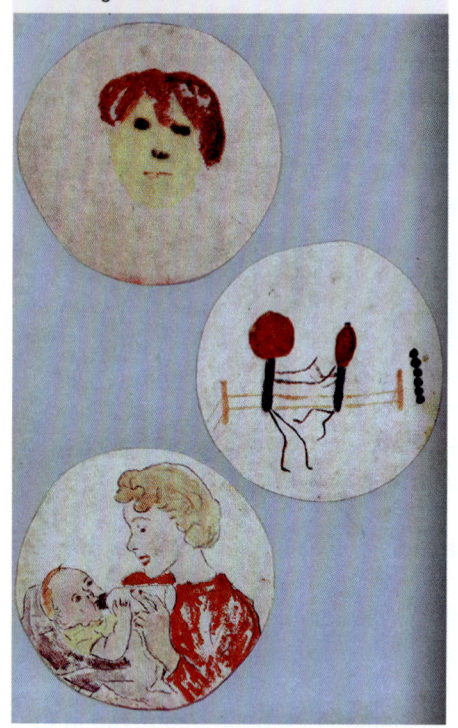

EXTEND YOUR KNOWLEDGE

Fleming was a member of the Chelsea Arts Club and he experimented in painting with microorganisms! He used microorganisms which had different natural colours; he would fill a Petri dish with agar jelly and 'grow' each culture. He would then 'paint' a picture using these cultures. However, the microorganisms continued to grow; over time, the cultures grew into each other so the sections of his painting were no longer clear.

In 1929, Fleming published his research into penicillin in the *British Journal of Experimental Pathology*. However, few people realised the importance of this discovery. Penicillin was difficult to produce – it was only possible to make small quantities at a time. Furthermore, laboratory tests suggested it was slow to act and ineffective when mixed with blood. Fleming thought it would work better as an external cream than an internal drug. He failed to get funding to continue this research and returned to his original work.

THE SECOND MAGIC BULLET

KEY TERMS

genus a group of similar types of microorganisms

antibiotic a drug using one type of bacteria (microorganisms) to fight the microorganisms causing the illness or the infection

Since the discovery of Salvarsan 606, scientists had been trying to develop another magic bullet that could be used to treat other illnesses. However, it was not until 1932 that the German scientist Gerhard Domagk tested Prontosil. This was based on a bright red chemical compound used to dye wool and leather. Domagk found that the chemical could be used to kill streptococcus infections in mice. In 1935, Domagk's 6-year-old daughter Hildegard became ill after an accident in which an embroidery needle had gone into her hand. She developed a fever, her hand became swollen and red stripes crept up her arm. Her doctor recommended amputating her arm but it was likely that she would die anyway, if the infection had poisoned her blood. Tests showed that the infection was caused by streptococcus. In desperation, Domagk gave Hildegard Prontosil, which completely cured her.

Domagk published his laboratory results, and tests in a British hospital showed that Prontosil could cure puerperal fever (a bacterial infection associated with childbirth). The key ingredient in Prontosil is sulphonamide; other sulphonamide drugs were now developed which could cure pneumonia, scarlet fever and meningitis.

FURTHER RESEARCH ON PENICILLIN BY FLOREY AND CHAIN

SOURCE C

From the acceptance speech made by Fleming when he was awarded the Nobel Prize in Medicine, 1945.

I isolated the contaminating mould. It made an antibacterial substance which I christened penicillin. I studied it as far as I could as a bacteriologist. I had a clue that here was something good but I could not possibly know how good it was and I had not the team, especially the chemical team, necessary to concentrate and stabilise the penicillin.

As Fleming noted in his speech in 1945 (Source C), no progress had been made in the development of penicillin because a chemist was needed to purify the mould. However, in 1939, a team at an Oxford hospital, led by Howard Florey and Ernst Chain, began to follow up on Fleming's research. Funds were limited and the skills of a biochemist, Norman Heatley, were very important; Heatley was able to construct equipment cheaply to purify penicillin.

Finally, in 1940, the team had purified enough penicillin to test it on mice.
- Eight mice were given enough streptococci to kill them.
- Four mice were also given penicillin.
- Within 16 hours, the four mice that had not been given penicillin had died.
- The mice that had been treated survived, for varying amounts of time.

The results of the experiment are shown in the tables below.

▼ MICE NOT TREATED WITH PENICILLIN

Mouse 1	Very sick 7 hours after infection	Survived for 12 hours
Mouse 2	Very sick 7 hours after infection	Survived for 14 hours
Mouse 3	Very sick 7 hours after infection	Survived for 14 hours
Mouse 4	Very sick 7 hours after infection	Survived for 16 hours

▼ MICE TREATED WITH PENICILLIN

Mouse 5	Given 10 mg of penicillin after 2 hours	Survived for 4 days
Mouse 6	Given 10 mg of penicillin after 2 hours	Survived for 6 days
Mouse 7	Given 5 mg of penicillin after 2 hours, 4 hours, 6 hours, 8 hours and 10 hours	Survived 13 days
Mouse 8	Given 5 mg of penicillin after 2 hours, 4 hours, 6 hours, 8 hours and 10 hours	Survived over 6 weeks

This was an exciting result. However, the team would need to produce 500 litres of the penicillin mould in order to purify enough penicillin to test on a human. Norman Heatley experimented with containers to find the best way to produce large quantities of the mould. He also employed six 'Penicillin Girls' to be responsible for the culture. By 1941, the team thought they had purified enough of the penicillin mould to test it on a human.

EXTEND YOUR KNOWLEDGE

The penicillin culture had to be grown on top of a liquid with a large surface area. Heatley and the other members of the team experimented with a range of containers, including pie dishes, biscuit tins and petrol cans. They found that hospital bedpans were particularly suitable as they had a large surface area; Heatley placed an order for 1,000 square bedpans. He also managed to mechanise the process, constructing a machine six feet (1.8 metres) tall, with a doorbell to signal when a bottle was full or empty.

TREATMENT USING PENICILLIN

In 1941, the team treated their first patient: Albert Alexander, a local policeman who had developed septicaemia after a scratch from a rose bush. His whole face, eyes and scalp had swollen. He had already had one eye removed and **abscesses** drained; his remaining eye was also badly swollen and painful. He was given penicillin and quickly began to recover – but the team ran out of penicillin! In desperation, they collected Alexander's urine every day and took it back to the laboratory to extract any penicillin that had passed through his body. Unfortunately, they could not produce enough penicillin to complete his treatment and he died.

The treatment of Albert Alexander had shown that penicillin had the potential to save lives. It had also shown that it was essential to find a way to manufacture large quantities of the drug. The team decided to use penicillin only on children, who would require smaller doses. Soon, children were being treated successfully. Florey refused to apply for a patent; he felt that penicillin was such an important drug, it should be available to everyone once they could mass-produce it.

ACTIVITY

1 Why did Fleming not develop penicillin for use in medicine?
2 Study the tables showing the results of the experiment using mice. What can you learn from this about the most effective way to use penicillin?
3 Explain why Norman Heatley was an important member of the research team.
4 Write a newspaper article or a report on the work of Florey and Chain. Summarise what they have proved about the use of penicillin in medicine and what was needed in the next stage of research and development.

MASS PRODUCTION

Florey knew the team needed funding and a large-scale factory to be able to grow and purify penicillin in large quantities. However, Britain had been at war since 1939 so there was very little funding available. Factories were either working on the war effort – producing supplies of existing drugs – or they had been damaged by bombs. Florey could not get enough support from **pharmaceutical** companies in Britain, so he decided to apply to companies in the USA. At that point, the USA was not involved in the war.

Florey's presentation about penicillin impressed key American scientists and 35 institutions became involved in the project. They included university chemistry departments, government agencies, research foundations and pharmaceutical companies. Their work led to various advances in growing and storing penicillin. These advances could be used both in the USA and in Britain. Once the USA entered the war in December 1941, large amounts of funding were committed to the development of penicillin.

SOURCE D

Manufacturing penicillin in Britain, November 1943. In each of these culture flasks, a single dose of penicillin is being made: 300 flasks are equal to 300 doses. It will be at least three weeks before the pure penicillin is extracted.

THE IMPORTANCE OF PENICILLIN

By 1943, Florey had enough penicillin to test its use on a larger scale. He travelled to North Africa, where penicillin was used to treat injured soldiers. The heat and conditions in North Africa meant that wounds often became infected; as a result, many soldiers had to have their limbs amputated. Florey suggested

ADVANCES, 1920–48 | CHANGES IN MEDICINE, c1848–c1948

EXTEND YOUR KNOWLEDGE

It is difficult to establish exact figures for the numbers of deaths and injuries in battle. It is estimated that there were 10,000 Allied casualties in the D-Day landings, including 2,500 killed in action. When the subsequent fighting in France is included, the number of Allied casualties rises to 210,000, with nearly 37,000 killed. It has been estimated that 15 per cent of the survivors were saved by the use of penicillin.

that wounds should be cleaned and the injured soldiers given penicillin. This was extremely effective.

The results of tests using penicillin were very convincing, and techniques for mass production were improving all the time. By 1944, there was enough penicillin available to treat all Allied casualties in the D-Day landings. The new antibiotic was used for military patients who had undergone major operations (including amputation) or who had extensive wounds. Penicillin was given by injection but it took time to prepare the wonder drug: the powder had to be mixed with sterile saline before it could be injected, and **syringes** had to be sterilised before they were reused.

The work of Fleming, Florey and Chain was important in the development of penicillin. However, their work would not have been successful without other factors, such as scientific knowledge, technological equipment and funding.

Institutions. The US government agreed to fund Florey's research for 5 years. This enabled him to develop methods to mass-produce the drug.

Technology. The development of new ways of mass-producing and storing penicillin made the drug available in vast quantities.

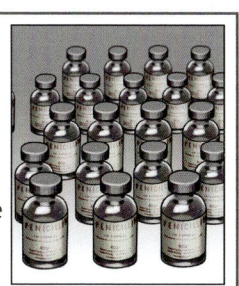

Individuals. Florey and Chain built on the work of Fleming. All three were actively looking for a chemical treatment for disease and illness. Florey also refused to patent the drug, saying that it should be available for everybody. This meant that developing it didn't cost as much money.

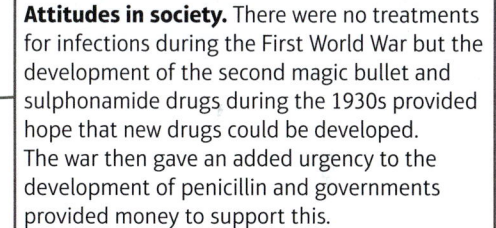

Main factors

Attitudes in society. There were no treatments for infections during the First World War but the development of the second magic bullet and sulphonamide drugs during the 1930s provided hope that new drugs could be developed. The war then gave an added urgency to the development of penicillin and governments provided money to support this.

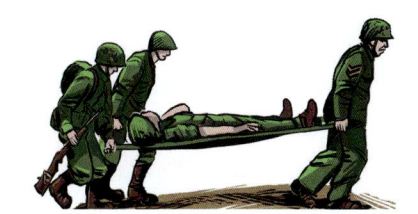

Science. Scientists were able to observe how penicillin attacked staphylococcus bacteria and this enabled them to modify it to attack other types of bacteria.

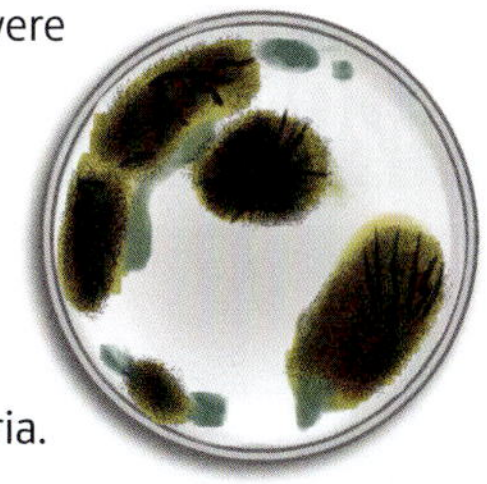

▲ Figure 5.1 The main factors that enabled the development of penicillin

NOBEL PRIZE

Sir Almroth Wright was the head of the department in which Fleming worked at St Mary's Hospital, London. In 1942, he wrote to the *Times* newspaper, complaining that Fleming's role in the discovery of penicillin had been overlooked. He claimed that Fleming had discovered penicillin and suggested that it might have important uses in medicine; these claims annoyed the Oxford team working on the development of penicillin.

SOURCE E
From a letter written by Howard Florey to the Medical Research Council, 19 June 1944.

We have been irritated to see the campaign carried on from St Mary's to credit Fleming with all the work done here at Oxford. He is being put over as 'the discoverer of penicillin' (which is true). But it is also suggested that he did all the work leading to its use in medicine (which is not true). My colleagues here are upset at seeing so much of their own work going to glorify someone else.

In 1945, the Nobel Prize for Medicine was awarded jointly to Fleming, Florey and Chain. Controversially, Heatley was not awarded a Nobel prize, but was recognised for his contribution many years later. It has been estimated that penicillin has saved at least 200 million lives since its first use as a medicine in 1942.

The success of penicillin led to further research, because it showed that one type of bacteria (penicillin) could be used to attack and kill another (streptococcus). Scientists carried out further research in this area. This led to the discovery that another mould could be used to make the drug streptomycin, which is effective in treating tuberculosis.

Some people are allergic to penicillin. However, further research was carried out by over 1,000 British and American scientists, working in 39 laboratories; this research cost $20 million. In 1955, a synthetic version of penicillin was produced.

ACTIVITY

1 Create a timeline of the key events in the discovery and development of penicillin.
2 Why was war an important factor in the development of penicillin?
3 Write a speech explaining why the Nobel Prize should have gone to Fleming alone, or just to Florey and Chain, or to all four contributors.

EXAM-STYLE QUESTION

A01 A02

SKILLS ADAPTIVE LEARNING

Explain **two** causes of improvement in treatment from 1905–48. **(8 marks)**

HINT
Make sure you explain each cause of improvement clearly. Describe an aspect of treatment that improved and explain why that change happened, giving details to support your comments.

5.2 THE IMPACT OF THE SECOND WORLD WAR

LEARNING OBJECTIVES

- Understand the impact of the war on the role of women in medicine
- Analyse the impact of the war on surgery
- Evaluate the importance of the war for progress in medicine.

In the period after the First World War, there were some important developments in medicine. Prontosil, a second magic bullet, had been developed. The Ministry of Health was created in 1919 and isolation hospitals were set up for tuberculosis patients. The government encouraged vaccination against diphtheria and tried to improve the health of children by providing free milk during the school day.

ADVANCES, 1920–48 | CHANGES IN MEDICINE, c1848–c1948

Advances in surgery which had begun during the First World War were developed further. Harold Gillies continued to work on plastic surgery; Harvey Cushing continued to work on brain surgery; and a blood transfusion service was developed by the British Red Cross and London Blood Transfusion Service. However, once the war was over there was still an expectation in some more traditional parts of medicine that women doctors would step aside to make way for male doctors or restrict themselves to the areas considered to be 'traditional women's medicine'.

However, there was less urgency now the war was over, and there was no central control of different organisations. Research teams, such as the one headed by Florey and Chain, often found it difficult to get funding and resources. Medical care was still provided mainly through GPs and small local hospitals. The larger hospitals and medical schools might be involved in developing new techniques, but the new ideas were slow to spread.

THE IMPACT OF THE WAR ON HOSPITALS IN BRITAIN

When war broke out in 1939, Britain had to deal with large numbers of injuries. The injured people included members of the armed forces fighting abroad, but many British civilians were wounded as well. When Britain was bombed, many people were hurt by the explosions, damaged buildings or fires.

It became important to co-ordinate voluntary or charity hospitals with the hospitals run by the town councils; it was also necessary to make sure there were enough ambulances and doctors in areas where bombing was expected. The Emergency Medical Service was created in 1939.

SOURCE F
Eileen Dunne, aged three, in Great Ormond Street Hospital, London, 1940. She was injured during the Blitz.

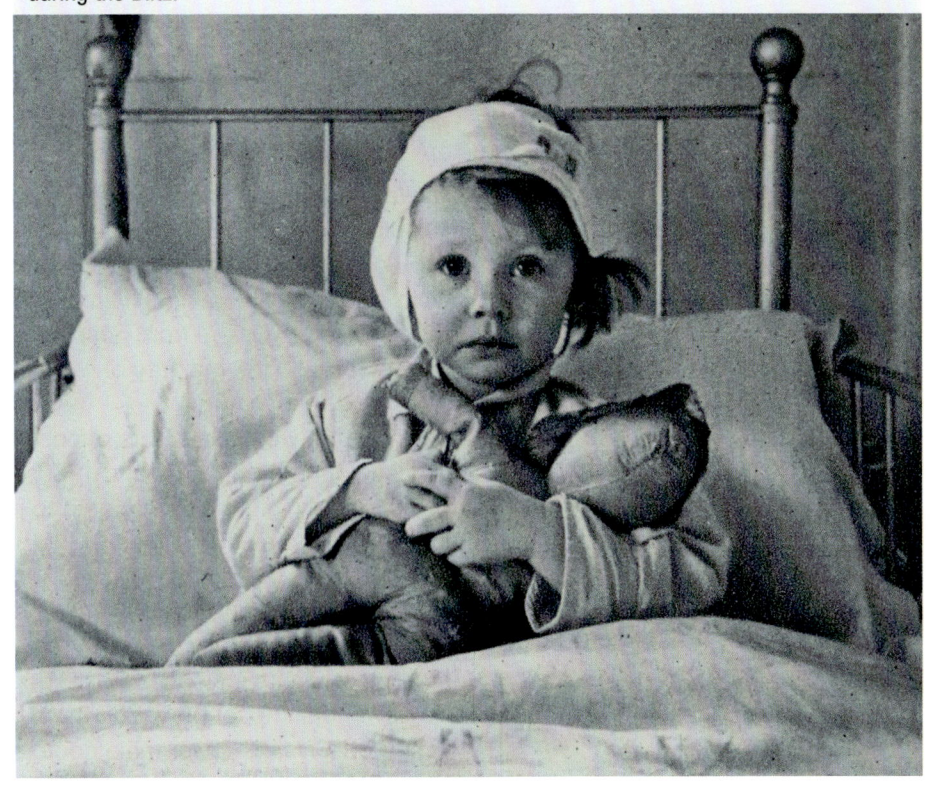

In London, plans had been drawn up before the war broke out; these plans divided an area of about 65 km into ten sections. The general aim was to establish first aid and casualty sorting centres in the danger areas. These centres would provide basic treatment so that casualties could be transported to better-equipped hospitals in safer areas. The first aid and casualty sorting centres were usually teaching hospitals, so doctors and nurses gained wide experience as they treated large numbers of varied injuries.

During the Second World War, the casualties from bombing put pressure on the hospitals, which might themselves have been damaged.
- A nurse at a hospital in south London described medical staff carrying buckets of sand and water to put out signal flares which were dropped to light up the area for the bombers.
- A bomb fell on the emergency hospital in Sutton, in 1940, killing 30 mothers and babies who had been evacuated from Guy's Hospital in London. In 1944, a hospital in south London received several direct hits, with two wards destroyed and 70 patients and staff injured; three died.

THE ROLE OF WOMEN

Before the First World War, women doctors had mainly been GPs or had worked in hospitals for women and children; there had been little opportunity to work in the big general hospitals where they could develop specialist skills and gain promotion. By 1931, approximately 10 per cent of the 30,000 doctors were women yet they still found it difficult to get jobs in general hospitals because they had finished their training after the war ended, when experienced male doctors had returned from war. So, in the period 1920–48, female doctors were still more likely to be GPs or to work in public health clinics than to be doctors in hospitals.

During the 1920s many medical schools discouraged female students from entering training or stopped admitting women altogether because:
- they thought training women was a waste as women would leave the profession to get married and raise a family
- some men believed medical training destroyed the 'delicate nature' of women
- some of the male students did not want to train alongside women.

However, a survey of 230 women who had entered training at St Mary's Hospital Medical School between 1916–24 showed that only 17 per cent were not working in medicine in 1936 (and almost a quarter were married, with children, yet still working full time). Nevertheless, women doctors often found themselves dismissed from hospital work when they married and this again tended to push the majority of women doctors into the role of GP.

The fact that women doctors often were paid less than male doctors became an issue during the 1920s and 1930s. Some men worried that if women were cheaper, they might be appointed to jobs ahead of men. This led to a number of hospitals agreeing salaries would be the same for both sexes.

The Second World War (1939–45) once again opened up opportunities for women to take on new roles and responsibilities and the number of female medical students increased from about 2,000 in 1938 to 2,900 in 1946. However, the impact of war on the medical profession was less than in the First World War as fewer male doctors were called up to serve in the armed forces. Many women doctors worked within the Emergency Medical Service, set up by the government to co-ordinate hospitals during the war, yet they were often sent to the smaller hospitals rather than working in the centre of the cities where there was most need for emergency care.

Evacuation also put pressure on the medical services: large hospitals were mainly in towns and cities but children were evacuated away from these areas, into the countryside. Here, there were fewer doctors and the hospitals often lacked extensive facilities. District nurses carried out medical examinations before children were evacuated, to see if any children needed special care, but the evacuated children from poor backgrounds often had health issues such as skin infections.

The medical services were helped by voluntary organisations. For example, the Red Cross set up first aid posts and mobile first aid units. This meant that the ambulance services could focus on the most urgent cases. Volunteers also acted as **stretcher** bearers and gave first aid to people pulled from the rubble. Source G shows members of the Red Cross working in a London underground station, where many people took shelter during bombing raids.

SOURCE G
British Red Cross staff examining patients in Piccadilly tube station.

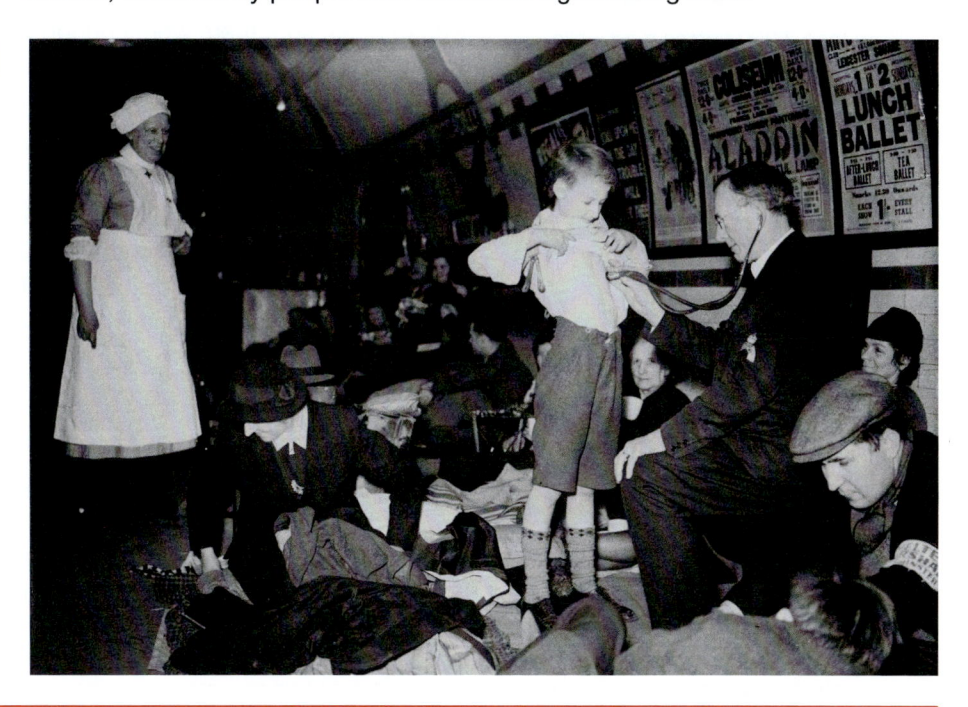

NURSES IN WAR ZONES

Many nurses served abroad with the army as part of the First Aid Nursing Yeomanry (FANY), Voluntary Aid Detachment (VAD), Territorial Army Nursing Service (TANS) and Queen Alexandra's Imperial Military Nursing Service (QAIMNS).

In 1938, there were about 500 QAIMNS working in military hospitals abroad. However, war seemed likely, so **matrons** in civilian hospitals (particularly teaching hospitals) often 'requested' suitable trained nurses to join the QAIMNS. These nurses were interviewed at the War Office and given a sealed packet, which had the instruction 'Open only in the event of war'. Towards the end of the war, as the British and American forces prepared to invade France in 1944, members of the QAIMNS had physical and military training; this included self-defence, how to climb a rope ladder on a ship, how to jump from a ship to a boat and how to move through barbed wire. By 1945, members of the QAIMNS had served in countries such as China, Egypt, Iceland and Italy.

ADVANCES, 1920–48 — CHANGES IN MEDICINE, c1848–c1948

EXTRACT A

An account taken from a website about the work of members of QAIMNS. This is describing an event in 1941, when the British army was escaping from a German attack at Dunkirk in France. A number of soldiers had been wounded and now needed to be transported back to Britain.

One of the last nursing sisters to leave France was Lillian Gutteridge, who bravely defended her patients. A German officer tried to take over her ambulance and ordered his men to throw out the stretcher-bound patients. Lillian Gutteridge was so angry that she slapped the officer's face. He stabbed her in the thigh with his dagger but he was killed by some British soldiers before he could hurt her anymore. Despite her wound, she drove the ambulance and her wounded patients to the railway siding and persuaded the French train driver to take her patients on board. They needed to travel to a port in order to cross the Channel and get back to England. During the train journey, they took on board another 600 French and British wounded troops. Several days later Lillian and her patients arrived safely in England.

Recruitment for army nurses to work in war zones overseas was so successful that, in 1943, it was decided that only newly qualified nurses could join. This was to make sure there were enough experienced nurses left in Britain to care for civilian air raid casualties.

EXTEND YOUR KNOWLEDGE

More than 2,000 nurses died while serving during the First and Second World Wars. In 2012, the Royal College of Nurses began a campaign for a memorial to be put up in honour of the role of nurses in war zones.

ACTIVITY

1. What types of medical care would be needed after a bombing raid?
2. How was the normal routine of a hospital affected by the war?
3. What can you learn from Source G about the work of the Red Cross?
4. If nursing in a war zone was so dangerous, why do you think so many nurses volunteered to do it?

THE IMPACT OF WAR ON SURGERY

During the First World War, doctors had realised that it was essential to clean wounds and give treatment as quickly as possible, in order to avoid gangrene. However, the average time gap between injury and an operation was 14 hours. Penicillin was particularly effective in preventing gangrene, so its mass production later in the war was a major factor in increasing survival rates.

PLASTIC SURGERY

The biggest advance in surgical techniques was in the development of plastic surgery. In 1920, Harold Gillies and T.P. Kilner published *Plastic Surgery of the Face*, based on their experiences of treating facial injuries during the First World War. This book became very influential and important. Gillies stressed the importance of working with dental and other medical experts; he travelled extensively, giving lectures and teaching about new techniques in plastic surgery. The importance of his work was officially recognised when he was knighted in 1930.

While working at St Bartholomew's Hospital, London, Gillies also set up a private practice dealing with cases of plastic surgery. In 1930, his relative, Archibald McIndoe, came from New Zealand to Britain. McIndoe joined Gillies and began to specialise in plastic surgery; he became the RAF consultant surgeon in 1938.

THE PROBLEM OF BURNS

When war broke out, there were only four fully experienced plastic surgeons in Britain. These surgeons were asked to head up four separate plastic surgery units. McIndoe headed the Blond McIndoe Research Centre, based at the Queen Victoria Hospital in East Grinstead, West Sussex. His work became famous early in the war, when he dealt with RAF pilots from the Battle of Britain.

Pilots often suffered terrible burns if their plane caught fire. Deep burns cause two main problems:
- muscles and **nerves** are damaged, so the patient is unable to move or feel the burned areas
- there is disfigurement to the patient's appearance, which often led to psychological problems.

The usual treatment for burns involved a chemical coating to protect the burned area. However, this chemical shrank the tissue around the burn. In large burns, this tightened the tissue, so the patient had less movement in the burned area. McIndoe noticed that the burns of pilots who had crashed into the sea seemed to heal better than those who had crashed on land; as a result, he banned the chemical treatment and began placing patients in saline baths instead.

SOURCE H

A patient in a saline bath. Notice the use of a face mask by the assistant to reduce the chance of infection.

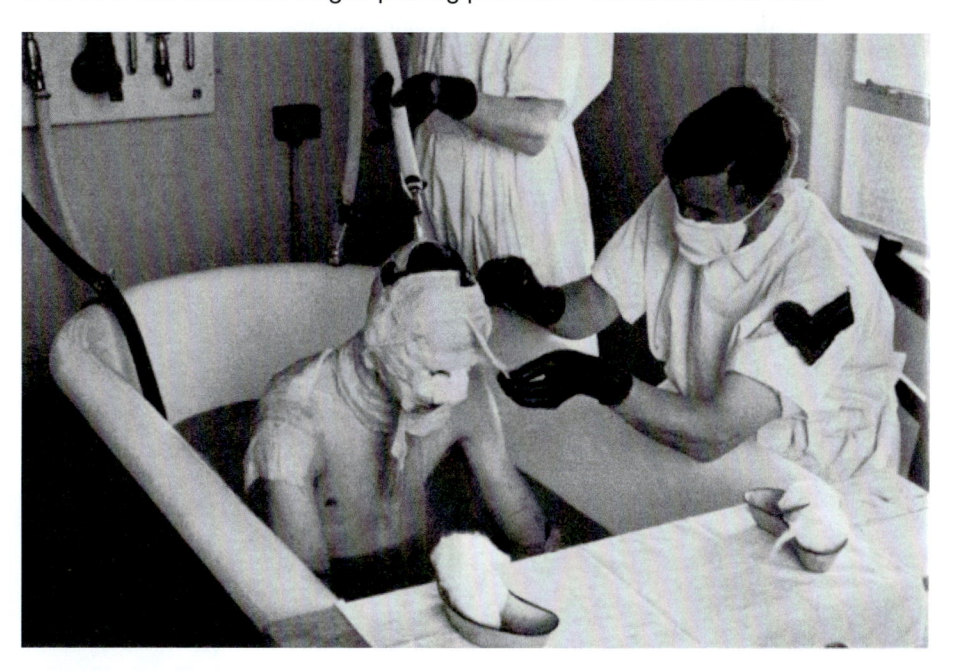

SKIN GRAFTS

In cases of severe damage, new skin may not be able to grow. A skin graft is a technique where a layer of skin is taken from an undamaged part of the body and transplanted to the damaged area. However, the transplanted tissue needs a good blood supply; otherwise, the graft will not grow in the new site. In 1916, a Ukrainian surgeon called Vladimir Filatov had developed pedicle skin grafts, growing flaps of skin that could be grafted onto another area of the body; this was similar to Gillies' work using pedicle tubes. Since the First World War, more work had been done on using small pieces of bone to rebuild features such as the nose. Filatov had also developed methods of grafts and **transplants** for the eyes, which meant that some patients could retain their sight. The scientist, Colebrook, was also researching ways of dealing with infection in burns.

THE GUINEA PIG CLUB

McIndoe's patients called themselves the 'Guinea Pig Club' because the use of new techniques in treatment was a process of trial and error: the methods being used were so new that no one could tell if they would work. Some patients had over 30 separate operations. There was an emphasis on keeping a positive mood – patients were encouraged to wear their uniform and walk around, a barrel of beer was kept on the ward and many patients smoked.

However, many patients suffered psychological problems: they had to adjust to their new appearance and there was a fear of rejection by society. Neville and Elaine Blond helped to deal with this by arranging for local families to welcome pilots into their homes. This helped the pilots to mix with the local community. Members of the Guinea Pig Club were welcomed in the local shops and pubs and East Grinstead became known as the village 'where no one stared'. McIndoe also arranged visits by famous people, and dancers from the London theatres, to let the men talk to young women again.

In 1947, McIndoe was knighted because of the importance of his work.

SOURCE I

A photograph from 1947, showing 'guinea pigs', nurses and McIndoe (seated near the piano wearing glasses).

ARCHIE McINDOE WITH GUINEA PIGS CHRISTMAS 1947

ACTIVITY

1. Why do you think patients were willing to go through so many operations even after their injuries had been treated?
2. How important do you think it was for the confidence of the patients to feel that people in the village would not stare at them, and to see that famous people and pretty girls would talk to them?
3. Do you think people would react differently to the appearance of the burned pilots if they met them in uniform, rather than normal clothes?

| ADVANCES, 1920–48 | CHANGES IN MEDICINE, c1848–c1948 | 101 |

> **EXTEND YOUR KNOWLEDGE**
>
> The patients often used humour to get through difficult situations. When the Guinea Pig Club was formed, the person chosen as secretary had badly burned fingers so he couldn't make detailed notes at the meetings. The treasurer was chosen because he had badly burned legs so he couldn't walk off with the club's money. Alan Morgan's fingers had been amputated and he remembers being called 'Fingers Morgan': 'There was another guy who lost all of his toes so I said to him "I'll play the piano and you do the tap dancing"'.

THE IMPACT OF THE WAR ON OTHER DEVELOPMENTS IN MEDICINE

The American surgeon, Harvey Cushing, had done important work on neurosurgery during the First World War. This was followed up by the British surgeon, Wylie McKissock. McKissock spent time in Sweden and the USA studying new techniques in neurosurgery; during the war he led a neurosurgical unit dealing with brain injuries.

Another American surgeon, Dwight Harken, developed a technique to remove bullets and shrapnel from the heart. He successfully carried out 130 of these operations without a single death occurring. This was important for the later development of heart surgery – many doctors thought this type of surgery was not possible.

During the war, the blood transfusion service developed into an efficient organisation, storing and delivering blood wherever it was needed. In 1938, when there were fears of war with Germany, Dr Janet Vaughan collected 50 bottles of blood donated by volunteers. This was the largest stock of stored blood in the whole of London at the time. Meanwhile, the Army Blood Supply Depot was set up in Bristol and four large blood banks for civilians were created around London; in 1940, eight regional centres were set up as well.

In total, over 700,000 donors gave blood during the war. Doctors also started to use **blood plasma** as a substitute for whole blood and a dried plasma package was developed; this made transportation and storage much simpler. When the **rhesus** blood group system was discovered in 1939, transfusions became even safer.

Tetanus is a disease caused when microorganisms enter a wound and get into the bloodstream. It causes painful muscle spasms, high temperature and a rapid heartbeat, often leading to death. Work on tetanus microorganisms had led to the development of a vaccine. At the Battle of Dunkirk in 1940, 17,000 vaccinated soldiers were wounded. Not one of them developed tetanus.

The condition of **post-traumatic stress disorder** (PTSD) had been seen during the First World War; at this time, it was known as 'shell shock'. Attitudes towards the condition varied: some people refused to believe it existed and insisted that the sufferers were pretending to have symptoms, because they were cowards. Some attempts at treatment had been made, including electric shock treatment. Other sufferers had simply been cared for at home or in mental asylums. The condition was better understood by the time of the Second World War and 18 psychiatric hospitals were set up to care for servicemen with mental health problems. Some of these hospitals were based in stately homes such as Cholmondeley Castle, to provide peaceful conditions. It was hoped that this would help the patients' recovery.

> **ACTIVITY**
>
> 1. Make a list of the ways the Second World War affected medicine and hospitals in Britain.
> 2. Explain how the war affected the role of women in medicine.
> 3. Explain how plastic surgery improved during the war.
> 4. Draw a spider diagram showing the effects of the war on other aspects of medicine and surgery.

ADVANCES, 1920–48 | CHANGES IN MEDICINE, c1848–c1948

EXAM-STYLE QUESTION

AO1 **AO2**

SKILLS PROBLEM SOLVING, REASONING, DECISION MAKING

How far were developments in science and technology responsible for changes in medicine from 1905–48?

You may use the following information to help you with your answer:
- magic bullets
- plastic surgery.

You **must** also use information of your own. **(16 marks)**

HINT

To answer a 'how far' question, you need to look at aspects of rapid or important change and aspects of limited change. You then need to weigh up both sides of the issue and come to a conclusion.

5.3 THE DEVELOPMENT OF THE NATIONAL HEALTH SERVICE (NHS)

LEARNING OBJECTIVES

- Understand the role of Beveridge and Bevan
- Analyse the features of the NHS
- Evaluate the importance of the NHS for progress in medicine.

During the war, the role of the government in health expanded again. In the late 19th century, the government had taken responsibility for general public health and hygiene, focusing on living conditions. Early in the 20th century, new laws had been passed giving the government a role in keeping individuals healthy. In the 1930s, the government had carried out a campaign to persuade parents to have their children vaccinated against diphtheria. The Emergency Medical Service, created in 1939, worked to co-ordinate hospitals and health care.

It therefore seemed natural for the government to plan ahead and consider how the country would be rebuilt after the war. William Beveridge had trained as a lawyer. He had advised Lloyd George on pensions and National Insurance, and had been involved in organising the movement of men to various jobs during the First World War. He then became director of the London School of Economics. He was, therefore, a respected figure and was asked to produce a report outlining ideas for the future.

In fact, Beveridge was not keen to take on this work – he would have preferred a more direct role in the war effort. However, it quickly became clear that this report would be of major significance.

THE BEVERIDGE REPORT, 1942

Beveridge's report identified five key problems, which he called the 'giant evils'. These were:
- want – the problems of poverty and not having enough money or food
- disease
- ignorance – lack of education, meaning people were unlikely to get better jobs or to develop a better understanding of society
- squalor – living in dirty and unhygienic conditions
- idleness – unemployment, meaning people were more likely to become depressed and possibly turn to alcoholism or crime.

He felt that the state had a duty to help and protect the people; he also believed the people had a responsibility to do what they could to improve things for themselves.

The Beveridge Report was a best-seller. A survey of public opinion found that 95 per cent of the population had heard of it and there was huge support for its proposals. Many people felt that the Beveridge Report would provide a much brighter future for society in Britain.

At the end of the war, in 1945, a Labour government was elected. The new prime minister, Clement Attlee, announced that a welfare state would be set up to protect the people 'from the cradle to the grave'. This meant everyone could have an acceptable standard of living. The welfare system would be paid for through National Insurance contributions made by employees and employers (as in the system set up by Lloyd George in 1911). The National Insurance Act 1946 provided old age pensions, maternity benefits and payments to the sick and unemployed.

Figure 5.2 Factors leading to the creation of the NHS

What led to the setting up of the NHS in 1948?

- During the Second World War children had been evacuated from cities to stay in the countryside. Many people were shocked by the poverty they had grown up in. People wanted to create a 'New World' with better conditions for all.
- By the mid-20th century, there was much more acceptance about the government being involved in people's lives.
- Significant medical breakthroughs meant that much more could be done for the sick.
- There had been a need to organise hospitals and medical staff during the Second World War.

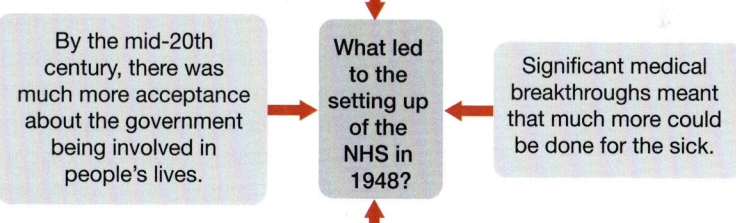

THE NATIONAL HEALTH SERVICE

A major step in establishing the welfare state was the introduction of the National Health Service. This brought all aspects of medicine and care into one organisation, under the government's control and paid for through the use of taxes. This was officially set up by the National Health Service Act, which was passed in 1946. As Figure 5.3 on page 105 shows, the care provided by the National Health Service began during pregnancy and at birth and continued throughout a person's life. It included medical diagnosis and treatment, access to a GP and to specialist consultants at hospitals, access to a dentist and ophthalmologist, emergency care and care for long-term illness or during old age.

ANEURIN BEVAN

The idea of the National Health Service was the result of Beveridge's report. However, the work of setting up the NHS was carried out by the Minister for Health, Aneurin Bevan. He came from a poor background in Wales, and had left school at the age of 13 to work in the local coal mine. He knew all about the problems of poverty and poor health, and became a trade union activist. He won a scholarship which paid for him to study in London. Then, in 1929, he became a Member of Parliament. As an MP, he continued to work to improve the lives of the poor.

When the new Labour government was elected in 1945, Bevan became Minister for Health, responsible for setting up the NHS. He faced a great deal of opposition from doctors, who did not like the idea that they would be employed by the NHS, instead of running their own private medical practices. Doctors did not receive much money for their hospital work and, as a result, they relied on the fees they got from private patients. In addition, many doctors were afraid they would lose money because they would not be able to set their own fees. A survey by the British Medical Association found that over 40,000 medical **practitioners** disapproved of the NHS Act, while fewer than 5,000 approved of it.

Eventually, Bevan agreed to pay GPs according to the number of patients they saw. He also agreed that GPs could continue to run their own private practices, as well as working for the NHS. A campaign to tell the public about the NHS encouraged people to put pressure on their doctors to join the NHS. Consequently, when the NHS came into operation in 1948, 90 per cent of the doctors in Britain had enrolled in the new system.

EXTRACT B

From Bevan's autobiography, published in 1952. Here, he explains that doctors were angry because they thought he wanted them to become part of the civil service, rather than being independent doctors. Since that was not part of his plan, he was able to let them 'win' that argument. This made it easier to get them to agree to other ideas.

The hardest task was overcoming the fears of the medical profession. It was easy for me to let them win victories because they had usually worked themselves up into a fever of protest against proposals which I had never made. They said they would never become civil servants. As I had never intended this I was able to give way without difficulty. They wanted patients to have a free choice of doctor. I myself wanted this.

The NHS was organised in three separate parts. Hospital services were brought into a single system and run by 14 regional boards. Doctors, dentists, opticians and pharmacists were employed through individual contracts; the GP played a key role, referring patients to hospital and writing **prescriptions** for medication. Local authority health services, led by the Medical Officer, ran maternity clinics, vaccination programmes and a school dental service. To begin with, everything was **free at the point of delivery**, paid for by National Insurance contributions and taxes.

ACTIVITY

1 Why do you think Bevan was so keen to make healthcare freely available to everyone?
2 Do you think Bevan tricked the doctors to get them to accept the NHS?

ADVANCES, 1920–48 — CHANGES IN MEDICINE, c1848–c1948

THE NEW NATIONAL HEALTH SERVICE

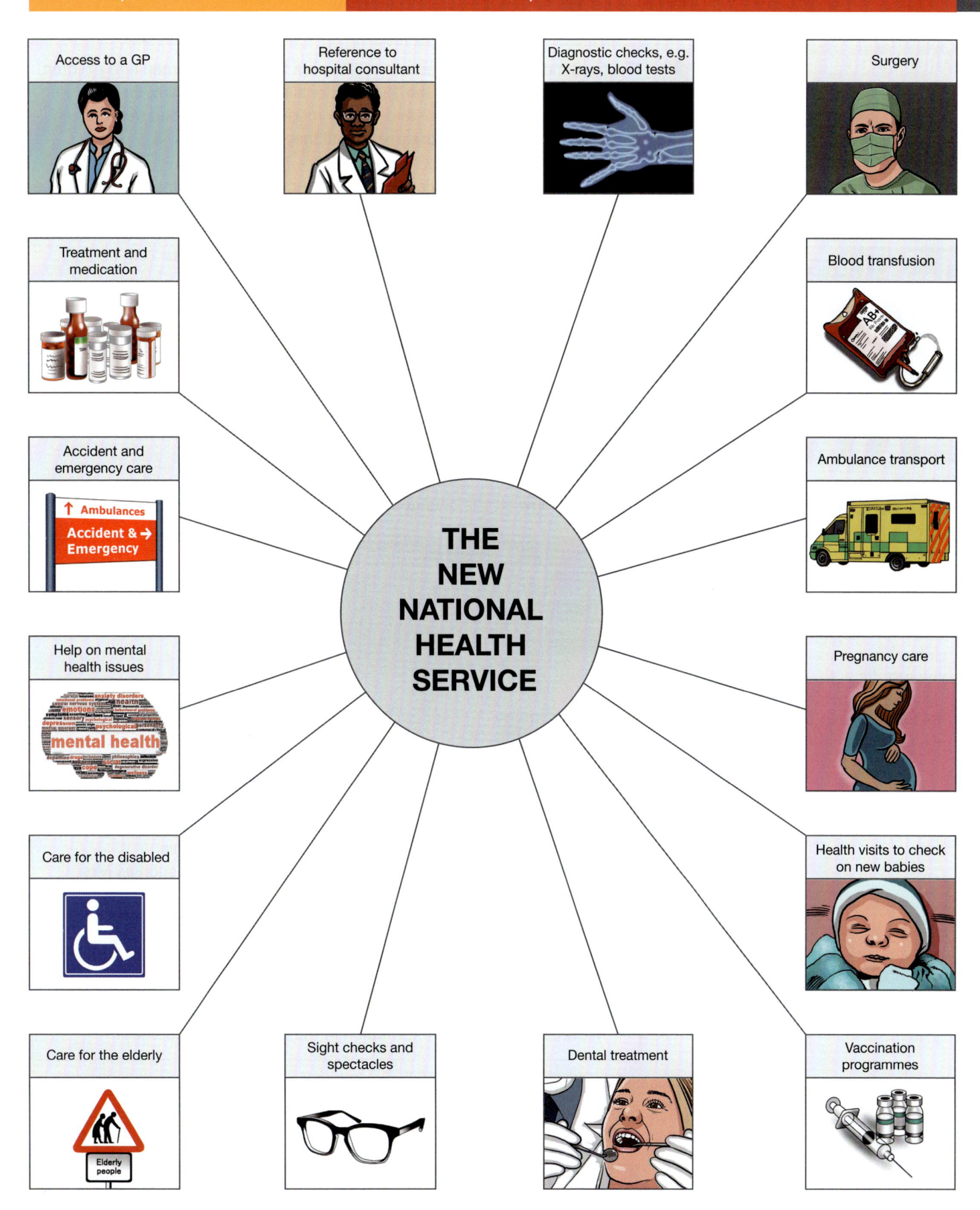

- Access to a GP
- Reference to hospital consultant
- Diagnostic checks, e.g. X-rays, blood tests
- Surgery
- Treatment and medication
- Blood transfusion
- Accident and emergency care
- Ambulance transport
- Help on mental health issues
- Pregnancy care
- Care for the disabled
- Health visits to check on new babies
- Care for the elderly
- Sight checks and spectacles
- Dental treatment
- Vaccination programmes

▲ Figure 5.3 The National Health Service

ADVANCES, 1920–48 — CHANGES IN MEDICINE, c1848–c1948

THE IMPACT OF THE NHS

SOURCE J

A photograph showing Aneurin Bevan visiting a patient at a Manchester hospital on the first day of the NHS, 5 July 1948. Bevan is accompanied by the matron of the hospital, who is in charge of the nurses.

EXTRACT C

From the recollections of Mrs Nora Leonard, speaking in 2000.

I think the NHS is just wonderful. Before it I never saw a doctor all the time I was pregnant with my first child. When you couldn't afford it, you just did without. I remember my father had cancer of the throat. The doctor lived next door to us. He sent his bill the day after father died.

The NHS made a huge difference to people's lives. Most women and children had not been protected by the 1911 National Insurance system; they had to pay for each visit to a doctor and for any medication prescribed. As a result, many people did not seek treatment until they were seriously ill.

The combination of the National Insurance Act and the National Health Service really did create a welfare state, in which the government offered support at every stage of life. Further developments in surgery, medicine and prevention, meant that **life expectancy** increased dramatically in the late 20th century.

The table below gives some figures about use of the NHS between July 1948 and October 1949. Bevan shared this information at a press conference in October 1949. The population of Britain at this point was about 50 million.

NUMBER OF PRESCRIPTIONS	187,000,000
SPECTACLES SUPPLIED	8,250,000
PATIENTS RECEIVING DENTAL TREATMENT	8,500,000

The table below shows changes in life expectancy between 1901 and 1950.

	MEN	WOMEN
1901	51	55
1930	58	62
1950	66	70

ACTIVITY

1. Explain the key ideas in the Beveridge Report.
2. Explain why the NHS was set up.
3. Create a table listing the different ways in which the National Insurance Act and the NHS helped children, women and old people.
4. Use Extract C to explain how the NHS affected people such as Mrs Leonard.
5. Why do you think so many pairs of spectacles were issued, and so much dental treatment was carried out, during the first year of the NHS?
6. The number of prescriptions issued suggests that some people needed several prescriptions, possibly to treat an ongoing illness or condition. How can you link this information to the rise in life expectancy?

EXAM-STYLE QUESTION

AO1 AO2

Explain **two** ways in which health care in 1905 was different from health care in 1948. **(6 marks)**

HINT

For each of the examples you give, make sure you describe the situation in 1905 and the situation in 1948, and then explain what the difference is.

RECAP

RECALL QUIZ

1. Who discovered penicillin as a result of his untidy laboratory habits?
2. Give one reason why it was difficult to use penicillin as a treatment.
3. Give two ways in which war affected the production of penicillin.
4. Who received the Nobel Prize for their work on penicillin?
5. Name one of the groups of nurses who worked with the armed forces during the war.
6. What was the Guinea Pig Club?
7. Give one way in which McIndoe improved plastic surgery for burned pilots.
8. Give one way that blood transfusions improved during the Second World War.
9. Name the five giant evils in the Beveridge Report.
10. Name five services the NHS provided from 1948.

CHECKPOINT

STRENGTHEN
S1 Explain why the mass production of penicillin was important.
S2 Explain why advances in plastic surgery were important during the war.
S3 Explain the ways in which the NHS gave improved medical care to most people.

CHALLENGE
C1 How important was Fleming's discovery of penicillin in 1928?
C2 How much did war lead to improvements in surgery?
C3 Why did many doctors oppose the introduction of the NHS?

SUMMARY

- Fleming discovered that penicillin, a microorganism, attacked other microorganisms such as staphylococcus.
- Florey and Chain led a research team which developed a method of mass production of penicillin.
- The government began to take more action on health, such as setting up isolation hospitals for tuberculosis patients and offering vaccinations for children against diphtheria.
- The Second World War meant that the government recognised the need to co-ordinate hospitals and medical services.
- Women's role as nurses was important, both in Britain and with the armed forces, but there was relatively little improvement in women's role as doctors.
- McIndoe developed new techniques in treating burns and reconstructive surgery.
- A blood transfusion service was set up for the war and further advances were made in the identification of the rhesus factor and the storage of blood.
- The Beveridge Report in 1942 identified the key problems that needed to be dealt with after the war.
- The National Insurance Act and the National Health Service were key elements of the new welfare state.
- The NHS offered access to a doctor, diagnosis, treatment and care, all free at the point of delivery.

EXAM GUIDANCE: PART (C) QUESTIONS

A01 **A02**

SKILLS PROBLEM SOLVING, REASONING, DECISION MAKING

Question to be answered: How far did medical treatment improve from 1905–48?

You may use the following in your answer:
- magic bullets
- the National Health Service.

You must also use information of your own. **(16 marks)**

1 Analysis Question 1: What is the question type testing?

In this question, you have to demonstrate that you have knowledge and understanding of the key features and characteristics of the period studied. In this particular case, you need to show your knowledge and understanding of improvements in medical treatment from 1905–48.

You also have to explain, analyse and make judgements about historical events and periods; here you need to give an explanation and reach a judgement about how much improvement there was in medical treatment.

2 Analysis Question 2: What do I have to do to answer the question well?

- You have been given two topics on which to write. You don't have to use them and can provide your own topics. (But it seems sensible to do so!)
- You must not simply give information. Think about how these examples show that there were improvements in medical treatment in this period.
- You are also asked 'how far' medical treatment improved. When discussing the developments in this period, you need to consider whether these improvements were significant or just minor changes. You are given two stimulus points to help you answer the question. One of these stimulus points may be about an area that supports and one which doesn't support the statement. But they might both be on the same 'side'. If so, it would be a good idea to find a third area from you knowledge which supports the opposite argument.
- The question says you must use information of your own. You should include at least one extra factor, beyond the two topics you have been given. For example, you could talk about the development and mass production of penicillin.

3 Analysis Question 3: Are there any techniques I can use to make it very clear that I am doing what is needed to be successful?

This is a 16-mark question and you need to make sure you give a substantial answer. You will be working against the clock so you may wish to use the following techniques to help you succeed.

- Don't write a lengthy introduction. Give a brief introduction which answers the question straight away and shows what your paragraphs are going to be about.
- Make sure you stay focused on the question and avoid just writing narrative. To help with this, try to use the words of the question at the beginning of each paragraph.
- Remember this question is about change over time. Make sure your answer explains whether each example was a major or minor change.

ADVANCES, 1920–48 | CHANGES IN MEDICINE, c1848–c1948

Answer
Here is a student response to the question. The teacher has made some comments.

Good introduction. →

There were some major improvements in medical treatment during the years 1905–1948. Salvarsan 606, the first magic bullet, was developed in 1909 and penicillin was discovered in 1928. However, Prontosil, the second magic bullet, was not discovered until 1932 and penicillin could not be mass-produced until 1943–44, so the biggest improvements in medical treatment were later in the period.

Nice paragraph. Answers the question, gives contextual knowledge and shows the importance of magic bullets as improvements in medical treatment. →

In 1905, there was no effective treatment for illness. Although the work of Pasteur and Koch had led to an improved understanding of illness, and vaccinations were being developed to prevent illness, there had been no developments in treatment. This means that Ehrlich's development of Salvarsan 606 was a major breakthrough – for the first time, an illness could be treated. Salvarsan 606 was developed to treat syphilis but it also showed the possibility of using chemicals to treat other illnesses. However, it took over 12 years before the second magic bullet was developed. Nevertheless, this was another major breakthrough – Prontosil could be used to treat blood poisoning, meningitis and pneumonia.

This is good detail, but there is no explanation to show why this was an improvement in medical treatment. You need to explicitly link the information here to the question about how far medical treatment improved. →

In 1928, Alexander Fleming investigated penicillin and found that penicillin microbes attacked other bacteria. He published his findings and, in the 1930s, Florey and Chain led a team to investigate penicillin further. They tested penicillin on mice and then on humans but they could not mass-produce it. However, they received help from the USA so that it was available by 1944.

This is a very disappointing paragraph. The NHS is one of the stimulus points and it was a major development in medical treatment at the end of the period in question. This is something students would be expected to know and discuss. →

During the Second World War, the Beveridge Report suggested that a National Health Service should be set up to make medical treatment and facilities available to everyone. Aneurin Bevan was the government minister responsible for carrying this out and the NHS was established in 1948.

Good concise finish; this makes a clear judgement about how far medical treatment had improved in this period. →

There were major improvements in the medical treatments available in the years 1905–1948. There were still some diseases which could not be treated and some conditions were genetic and not properly understood. However, treatment improved hugely from being very poor in 1905 to being effective against a range of illnesses in 1948. The NHS also meant that treatment became available to the whole population.

What are the strengths and weaknesses of this answer?
The teacher comments show strengths and weaknesses. Notice that the weaker second half of the answer has lots of detail but this detail is not used to answer the question. If there had been three paragraphs like the one about the development of magic bullets, this would have been a very good answer.

Work with a friend
Discuss with a friend how you would rewrite the weaker paragraphs in this answer so that the whole answer could get very high marks.

Challenge a friend
Use the Student Book to set a similar part (c) question for a friend. Then look at the answer. Does it do the following things?

☐ Identify improvements
☐ Provide detailed information about the improvements
☐ Consider examples that challenge the idea of improvement
☐ Provide an example other than the two given in the question
☐ Address 'how far?'

GLOSSARY

abscess a painful swollen part of your skin or inside your body that has become infected and is full of a yellowish liquid

acne a medical problem which causes a lot of red spots on your face and neck; it mainly affects young people

addictive if a substance, especially a drug, is addictive, your body starts to need it regularly and you are unable to stop taking it

agar jelly a jelly-like material, made from algae, in which bacteria and fungi can be grown

alloy a metal that consists of two or more metals mixed together

amputate cut off someone's arm, leg, finger etc. during a medical operation

anaesthetic a drug that stops you feeling pain

appendicitis an illness in which your appendix swells and causes pain

artery one of the tubes that carries blood from your heart to the rest of your body

arthritis a disease that causes the joints of your body to become swollen and very painful

authorities the national authority is the central government in London, based in the Houses of Parliament; local authorities are town and city councils

bacteria very small living things, some of which cause illness or disease

bedpan a wide container, shaped like a toilet seat, used for patients who cannot get out of bed to go to the toilet

bile the watery liquid that is part of vomit

blood plasma the yellowish liquid part of blood that contains the blood cells

blood type one of the classes into which human blood can be separated, including A, B, AB and O

blood vessel one of the tubes through which blood flows in your body

boil (n) a painful infected swelling under someone's skin

campaign (v) lead or take part in a series of actions intended to achieve a particular social or political result

carbolic acid a liquid that kills bacteria, used to prevent the spread of disease or infection

casualty someone who is hurt or killed in an accident or war

central nervous system the main part of your nervous system, consisting of your brain and your spinal cord

cesspool a hole in the ground for human waste to be collected; cesspools should have been emptied regularly but often they were not

chlorine a greenish-yellow gas with a strong smell

chloroform a liquid that makes you become unconscious if you breathe in the fumes

cholera a serious disease that causes sickness and sometimes death; caused by eating infected food or drinking infected water

clot become thicker and more solid

cocaine a drug, usually in the form of a white powder, that is used in some medical situations to prevent pain

compound a substance containing atoms from two or more elements

contaminate make a place or substance dirty or harmful by putting something such as chemicals or poison in it

diabetes a serious disease in which there is too much sugar in your blood

diagnose find out what illness someone has, after doing tests, examinations etc.

diarrhoea an illness in which waste from the bowels is watery and comes out often

diphtheria a serious infectious throat disease that makes breathing difficult

dissection cutting open a dead body in order to study the structure of bones, muscles and nerves, or the internal organs such as the heart, lungs, liver etc.

dissolve break down to become part of a liquid – like sugar dissolves in tea

donor someone who gives blood or a body organ so that it can be used in the medical treatment of someone else

Dressing Station a place for giving emergency medical treatment to soldiers who were injured in battle

dysentery a serious disease of your bowels that makes them bleed and pass much more waste than usual

empire a group of countries controlled by one ruler or government

enzyme a chemical substance that is produced in a plant or animal, and helps chemical changes to take place in the plant or animal

epidemic rapid spread of disease, affecting large numbers of the population

epilepsy a medical condition affecting your brain, that can make you suddenly become unconscious or unable to control your movements for a short time

GLOSSARY — CHANGES IN MEDICINE, c1848–c1948

ether a clear liquid used in the past as an anaesthetic to make people sleep before an operation

excrement human waste: faeces and urine

free at the point of delivery the patient does not have to pay for NHS services because these services are funded by the government, paid for from taxes

fumes a kind of smoke or steam in the air

gas gangrene a type of gangrene in which bacteria produce a foul-smelling gas in the affected parts of the body

germs very small living things that can make you ill, such as bacteria

GP general practitioner; a doctor who is trained in general medicine and treats people in a particular area or town

harassment when someone behaves in an unpleasant or threatening way towards you

hygiene the practice of keeping yourself and the things around you clean in order to prevent disease

hygienic clean and likely to prevent bacteria, infections, or disease from spreading

hypodermic needle a thin needle, which can be inserted under the skin to take a measured amount of blood or give a measured injection

hysterical unable to control your behaviour or emotions because you are very upset, afraid, excited etc.

infected a part of your body or a wound that is infected has harmful bacteria in it which prevent it from healing

infirmary a hospital

influenza a disease that creates a fever lasting three to five days, sometimes with vomiting or diarrhoea; this often led to death if the sufferer was already weak or in poor health

inhale breathe in air, smoke or gas

inject put liquid, especially a drug, into someone's body by using a hypodermic needle

intervention the act of becoming involved in an argument, fight or other difficult situation in order to change what happens

isolation hospital a special hospital for people with contagious or infectious diseases

leukaemia a type of cancer of the blood that causes weakness and sometimes death

lice small insects that live on the hair or skin of people or animals

license (v) give official permission for someone to do or produce something, or for an activity to take place

life expectancy the length of time that a person or animal is expected to live

limb an arm or leg

matron a nurse who is in charge of the other nurses in a hospital

mechanism part of a machine or a set of parts that does a particular job

medication medicine or drugs given to people who are ill

membrane a very thin piece of skin that covers or connects parts of your body

meningitis a serious illness in which the outer part of the brain becomes swollen

microbes/microorganisms extremely small living things which you can only see if you use a microscope; some microbes can cause disease

microscope a scientific instrument that makes extremely small things look larger

midwifery the skill or work of a midwife (a person who helped women during childbirth)

mould a soft green, grey or black substance that grows on food which has been kept too long, and on objects that are in warm wet air

muscle spasm an occasion when your muscles suddenly become tight, causing you pain

nerves parts inside your body which look like threads and carry messages between the brain and other parts of the body

nutrition the process of giving or getting the right type of food for good health and growth

open wound an injury such as a cut that might allow infection into the body

operating theatre a room in a hospital where operations are done

opium a powerful illegal drug made from poppy seeds; its legal use as a drug in medicine helps to reduce severe pain

outbreak a sudden occurrence of something unpleasant, such as illness

outpatient someone who goes to a hospital for treatment but does not stay for the night

pasteurise a liquid that is pasteurised has been heated using a special process in order to kill any harmful bacteria in it

penicillin a type of medicine that is used to treat infections caused by bacteria

pharmaceutical relating to the production of drugs and medicines

physician a doctor

plastic surgery the medical practice of changing the appearance of people's faces or bodies, either to improve their appearance or to repair injuries

pneumonia a serious illness that affects your lungs and makes it difficult for you to breathe

post-traumatic stress disorder a mental illness which can develop after a very bad experience such as a plane crash

poverty line a minimum standard of living where any unexpected event can send a family into poverty; this might be an illness which causes a loss in earnings or where a doctor needs to be paid

practitioner someone practising medicine

prescription a piece of paper on which a doctor writes what medicine a sick person should have, so that they can get it from a pharmacist

prosthetic limb an artificial leg or other part of the body which takes the place of a missing part

pus a thick yellowish liquid produced in an infected part of your body

rabies an infection that targets the brain and nervous system and often results in death; it is usually spread to humans by a bite from an infected animal

radiation a form of energy that comes especially from nuclear reactions; in large amounts, it is very harmful to living things

rhesus the rhesus factor of blood (positive or negative) depends on whether a specific protein is found in your red blood cells; you may have a reaction to a blood transfusion if the rhesus factor is not the same

ringworm a skin infection that causes red rings, especially on your head

sanitary relating to the ways that dirt, infection and waste are removed, so that places are clean and healthy for people to live in

sanitation having access to clean water for washing, drinking and cooking; having sewers for human excrement to be removed

scarlet fever a serious infectious illness that mainly affects children; it causes a sore throat and red spots on the skin

septicaemia blood poisoning, where large amounts of bacteria enter the bloodstream; it was often fatal

sewage a mixture of waste from the human body and used water

sewer a pipe or passage under the ground that carries away waste material and used water from houses, factories etc.

shrapnel bits of metal from an explosive bomb, often causing several wounds

side effect an effect that a drug has on your body in addition to curing pain or illness

smallpox a serious disease that often resulted in death or left the victim disfigured

solution a liquid in which a solid or gas has been mixed

stagnant water water that does not move or flow and often smells bad

staphylococcus a type of microorganism that can cause a range of infections, from a sore throat or boils on the skin to infection, pneumonia and blood poisoning; these infections can sometimes lead to death

sterilise kill microbes through the use of heat

stretcher a long piece of canvas with wooden poles at the side, used to carry someone who is too injured or ill to walk

stroke if someone has a stroke, an artery in their brain suddenly bursts or becomes blocked; the person may die or be unable to use some muscles

surgery medical treatment in which a surgeon cuts open your body to repair or remove something inside

syphilis a disease which produces spots, a fever, small skin growths, and pain; in the later stages, it can affect the brain before the patient dies

syringe an instrument for taking blood from someone's body or putting liquid, drugs etc. into it; a syringe consists of a hollow plastic tube and a needle

tetanus a serious illness caused by bacteria that enter your body through cuts and wounds; tetanus makes your muscles, especially your jaw, go stiff

transfusion the process of putting blood from one person's body into the body of someone else as a medical treatment

transplant move an organ, piece of skin etc. from one person's body and put it into another as a form of medical treatment

trench foot painful swelling of the feet, caused by standing in cold mud and water; trench foot could lead to gangrene

tuberculosis a serious infectious disease that affects many parts of the body, especially the lungs

unhygienic hygienic means clean and free from microorganisms; unhygienic means the opposite – dirty and likely to carry microorganisms

vaccination injecting weakened disease microorganisms into the body, so that it develops resistance to the disease in the future

vomit this word can mean to be sick and 'throw up' or it can mean what you produce when you are sick; 'vomited' means 'was sick'

welfare state a system in which the government provides money, free medical care etc. for people who are unemployed, ill, or too old to work

Western Front an area on Germany's western border with France where most of the fighting involving British soldiers took place

wound an injury to your body that is made by a weapon such as a knife or a bullet

X-ray a beam of radiation that can go through solid objects and is used for photographing the inside of the body; a photograph of part of someone's body, taken using X-rays, to see if anything is wrong

INDEX

A
Advanced Dressing Stations 74, 75
ambulance trains 76
amputation 8, 9, 10, 28, 73, 77, 81, 92
anaesthetics 2, 10, 13, 52–53, 78, 82
anthrax vaccine 47, 48, 49
antiseptics 23, 26, 28–9, 46, 47, 50, 61, 89
antitoxins 57, 58
army nurses 97–98
Artisans' Dwellings Act (1875) 54
aseptic surgery 46, 51, 61
attitudes 5, 29, 49, 60, 61, 93
    to public health 17–18, 32, 33, 55, 61, 66–7
    to women in medicine 38–42, 78, 96
Attlee, Clement 103

B
bacteriology 48, 60, 61, 89
Base Hospitals 75, 77, 79
Bazalgette, Joseph 19, 31, 53, 54
Behring, Emil von 57, 58
benefit payments 67, 69, 103
Bevan, Aneurin 103–4, 106
Beveridge, William (Beveridge Report) 102–3
'Black Period' (surgery) 12, 27
Blackwell, Elizabeth 39, 42
blood groups (types) 46, 56, 61, 80, 101
blood loss 9, 12, 13, 29, 52, 80
blood storage 57, 80, 88, 101
blood transfusions 56–7, 61, 80, 95, 101
brain surgery (neurosurgery) 82, 88, 95, 101
British Medical Association 41, 104
Broad Street pump 18–19
burns treatment 98–100

C
carbolic acid (spray) 27, 28, 29, 50, 51, 52
Carrel-Dakin method 81
Casualty Clearing Stations 74, 75, 77, 79, 81
catgut ligatures 52
Chadwick, Edwin 2, 16–17, 31, 32
Chain, Ernst 91, 93, 94
children's health and welfare 32, 36, 67–8, 94, 97, 102, 106
Chisholm, Mairi 77
chlorine gas 71, 72
chloroform (inhaler) 10–13, 27, 52
cholera 6, 14, 15–16, 17, 18–19, 28, 31, 47, 48, 49
cocaine 52
cottage hospitals 35
courts 14, 15, 16
Craiglockhart Hospital 73
cultures (bacteria) 47, 48, 57, 89–90, 91
Curie, Marie 60, 76, 79
Cushing, Harvey 82, 95, 101

D
diphtheria 55, 57
dissections 3, 4–5, 39, 40
doctors 5, 29, 49, 60, 61, 69, 77–9, 80, 95–6, 104
    training 3, 4–5, 8, 39, 40
    see also GPs; physicians
Domagk, Gerhard 90
Dressing Stations 74, 75, 81
dysentery 48, 73

E
Ehrlich, Paul 58
Emergency Medical Service 95, 102
ether 2, 10, 13
exam guidance 21–2, 44–5, 63–4, 86–7, 108–9
excision (debridement) 81
experiments (research) 47–9, 60, 61, 75, 89–91, 93, 94, 100–1

F
Filatov, Vladimir 99
first aid (First Aid Nursing Yeomanry) 76, 95, 96, 97
First World War 65, 71–84, 102
Fleming, Alexander 89–90, 91, 93–4
Florey, Howard 91, 92–4
folk remedies 69
Food and Drugs Act (1875) 54–5
Four Humours 3–4
funding 5, 7, 47, 48, 91, 92, 93, 95

G
gangrene 13, 71, 73, 81, 89, 98
Garrett Anderson, Elizabeth 23, 39–41, 42
Garrett Anderson, Louisa 77, 78
germ theory 19, 23, 24–6, 29, 47, 49, 50, 61
Gillies, Harold 82–3, 95, 98
government 5, 8, 23, 31–4, 46, 48, 55, 61, 65–87, 88
GPs 35, 78, 95, 96, 103, 104
    see also doctors; physicians
Great Ormond Street Hospital 36, 37, 38
Great Stink 19, 31
Guinea Pig Club 100–1

H
Harken, Dwight 101
health visitors 68
Heatley, Norman 91, 94
Hoggan, Frances 41, 42
hospitals 34–8, 40, 41, 59, 69, 75, 77–9, 95–6, 101, 104
    see also Craiglockart Hospital; isolation hospitals; King's College Hospital; Park Hospital; Scutari hospital; teaching hospitals
housing (living conditions) 2, 14–15, 16–17, 32, 46, 66, 67, 68
hygiene 4, 6–8, 9, 13, 16–17, 27, 28, 32, 36–8, 67–8

I
Industrial Revolution 14
infection 6, 9, 12–13, 27–8, 73, 75, 81, 89, 90
infectious diseases 14, 15–16, 47, 55, 57, 58, 101
    see also cholera; tuberculosis
Inglis, Elsie 77
isolation hospitals 55, 94
Ivens, Frances 77

J
Jex-Blake, Sophia 41, 42

K
King's College Hospital 37, 50, 90
Knocker, Elsie 77
knowledge 4–5, 55–6, 57, 61, 80
Koch, Robert 46, 47–9, 50, 57, 60

L
Labour Exchanges 68

Lancet, The 3, 42
Landsteiner, Karl 56, 80
life expectancy (1901-50) 106
Lister, Joseph 23, 27–30, 47, 50–2, 90
Liston, Robert 9, 10, 11
living conditions (housing) 2, 14–15, 16–17, 32, 46, 66, 67, 68
local anaesthetic 52, 53, 82
local authorities (councils) 15, 32, 33, 53, 54, 55–6, 67, 68, 104
London sewer system 31–2

M
magic bullet 58, 90, 94
McIndoe, Archibald 98, 99, 100
McKissock, Wylie 101
Medical Act (1876) 77
miasma 2, 4, 7, 15–16, 24, 36
microbes (microorganisms) 4, 19, 24–6, 27, 28–9, 47–8, 49, 57, 90
microscopes 5, 23, 24, 47, 49
mobile X-ray units 60, 77, 79, 80
Murray, Flora 77, 78
mustard gas 71

N
National Health Service 102–6
National Insurance Act (1911) 69
National Insurance Act (1946) 103, 106
neurosurgery (brain surgery) 82, 88, 95, 101
Nightingale, Florence 2, 6–8, 23, 28, 36–8, 39
Nobel Prize 93–4
nursing 6–8, 34–8, 65, 76, 77, 78, 96–8

O
Old Age Pensions Act (1908) 68

P
pain relief *see* chloroform; cocaine; ether; local anaesthetic
Park Hospital 55
Pasteur, Louis 19, 23, 24–6, 46, 47–9, 51, 60, 90
Pechey, Edith 41, 42
pedicle tube (skin grafts) 83, 99
penicillin 88, 89–94, 98
petri dishes 48, 90
phosgene gas 71, 72
physicians 11, 35, 40, 41
    see also doctors; GPs
plastic surgery 82–4, 88, 95, 98
poison gas 71–2, 81
post-traumatic stress disorder (shell shock) 73, 101
poverty 66, 67, 68, 69, 102
Prontosil 90, 94
prosthetic limbs 82, 88
public health 14–19, 23, 26, 31–4, 61, 65–87, 102–6
Public Health Act (1848) 16–17, 31
Public Health Act (1875) 23, 32–3, 46, 53–6, 61
published works 3, 36, 37, 47, 48–9, 90, 98

Q
Queen Alexandra's Imperial Nursing Service (QAIMNS) 76, 97

R
radiation 46, 60
Red Cross 95, 97
Regimental Aid Posts 74, 75
research (experiments) 47–9, 60, 61, 75, 89–91, 93, 94, 100–1
River Pollution Prevention Act (1876) 54, 55
Röntgen, Wilhelm 59
Royal Army Medical Corps (RAMC) 75–6, 78
Royal Free Hospital 36, 79

S
saline baths 99
Salvarsan 606 58, 73
Sanitary Act (1866) 32, 53
school meals 67
School Medical Service 68
Scutari hospital 6–8
Second World War 88, 92–102, 103
sewers 15, 17, 19, 31–2, 53, 55
shell shock 73, 101
sick clubs 69
Simpson, James 2, 10–11, 28
skin grafts 82–3, 99
Snow, John 2, 12, 18–19, 28, 31
Society of Apothecaries 40, 41
spontaneous generation 4, 24–5
steam sterilisers 50
Stobart, Mabel 77
surgery 8–13, 27–30, 50–3, 61, 69, 79–84, 82, 88, 95, 98–101
    see also amputation
surgical clothes 51, 53

T
taxes 16, 17, 32, 53, 67, 68, 103, 104
teaching hospitals 3, 39, 78–9, 96, 97
technology 5, 54, 55, 57, 60, 61, 93
    see also microscopes; X-rays
Theory of Opposites 3–4
Thomas splint 81–2
toilets 14, 33, 72, 73
tourniquets 9, 13
trench fever 73
trench foot 72, 73
tuberculosis 48, 49, 55, 59, 69, 94
tumours 8, 59, 60

U
USA 92, 93

V
vaccinations 26, 32, 46, 47–8, 49, 94, 101
Voluntary Aid Detachments (VADs) 76, 78, 97
voluntary hospitals 77
voting rights 32, 33, 39

W
water supply 7, 8, 14, 18–19, 32, 54, 55, 73
welfare state 67
Western Front 71–2, 73, 74, 75, 76, 77, 78, 79, 82
women in medicine 23, 38–42, 60, 65, 76–9, 95, 96–8
Women's Army Auxiliary Corps 76

X
X-rays 59, 60, 61, 77, 79–80